Minority Verdict

The Conservative Party, the voters
and the 2010 election

Michael A. Ashcroft

First published in Great Britain in 2010 by
Biteback Publishing Ltd
Westminster Tower
3 Albert Embankment
London
SE1 7SP

ISBN 978-1-84954-082-7

10 9 8 7 6 5 4 3 2 1

A CIP catalogue record for this book is available from the British Library.

Set in Garamond by SoapBox
Printed and bound in Great Britain by dg3

Contents

Introduction

THE RESULT of the 2010 general election was closer than many people expected. Certainly it was closer than Conservatives hoped it would be. With 306 seats in the House of Commons, the Conservative Party was twenty seats short of the overall majority that looked all but assured only weeks before polling day.

Even this tally was precarious. If a handful of results had gone the other way, the maths would have looked very different. The Conservatives won 32 seats that required a swing greater than the 4.9 per cent that they achieved nationally from Labour or the 1.4 per cent from the Liberal Democrats. Had they not done so, Labour would have remained the largest party in the Commons and would almost certainly have continued in office.

Many Conservatives were disappointed with the result. The party faced a shambolic government, an unpopular Prime Minister, a recession, a huge budget deficit and an overwhelming national desire for change. A year before the election they had been twenty points ahead in the polls. Surely this was an open goal. How could they come so close to missing?

To see the result simply as a failure is to underestimate the scale of the challenge the Conservatives faced at this election – and also, it must follow, the scale of what they achieved. The elections of 2005, 2001 and 1997 produced, in descending order, the Conservative Party's three worst ever results. The Conservatives had never before managed to return to government from a position as weak as the one they faced in 2010.

For a majority in the House of Commons the Conservatives needed to gain 117 seats in addition to the ones they already held. This would be by far the highest number of gains since 1931 (under the rather different circumstances of the National Government and the Labour schism that saw 210 Conservative gains with 55 per cent of the popular vote. The highest number of Conservative gains in a "normal" election was 87, in 1950 – in 2010 they needed a third as many again.)

An overall majority would need a uniform swing from Labour of 6.9 per cent – again, the highest the party would have achieved since 1931, and far greater than the 5.3 per cent achieved by Margaret Thatcher in 1979. The Conservatives needed to gain seats and swing the popular vote on a scale that had been achieved only once since 1945 – by Tony Blair and New Labour in 1997.

All this needed to be done on electoral geography that remained chronically skewed towards Labour. For any given vote share, Labour would win more seats than the Conservatives. The unfairness of this was such that at the 2005 election, Labour won 92 more seats in England than the Conservatives, despite coming second in the popular vote. Boundary changes since then would mean an extra 12 seats or so for the Conservatives and seven fewer for Labour – a very small impact given the scale of the imbalance. The effect of this continuing bias was that to achieve a majority of one seat in the House of Commons the Conservatives would need a double-digit lead in the popular vote (while in 2005 Labour had secured a majority of 66 while being ahead on vote share by just 3 points.)

Of course, any electoral system will seem unfair to somebody. But the fact remains that there was nothing inevitable about the Conservatives winning the 2010 general election. The political cycle is often described as a pendulum, with power swinging between one party and another as though it were governed by the laws of physics. But politics in Britain is not like a pendulum at all. Politicians are not elected and defeated by gravity, and governments do not lose just because their time is up. If parties want the pendulum to move, they have to push it themselves.

Seen in its proper perspective, the 2010 election result is an achievement of historic proportions for David Cameron and the Conservative Party. They did not manage an overall majority. But with 96 gains, they did achieve their best result since 1931 – or, if you consider the extraordinary circumstances of that year, the best Conservative result ever.

Yet I, too, was disappointed with it. I think that if the Conservatives had done certain things differently – not just during the campaign – we could have won more votes and more seats. It is important not to draw the wrong conclusions, however. One theory is that we did not achieve a majority because we failed to nail Labour on their record, wrongly chose not to highlight immigration, and talked too much about ourselves. It would be a disaster if this theory were to become the orthodoxy because it is wrong in every particular.

This election was about change. The overwhelming majority of voters thought it was time for change – 82 per cent in one survey three months before polling day – yet only 36 per cent voted Conservative. If we had talked even more about Labour's record than we did (and we talked about it endlessly), the very most we could have achieved was to add to a desire for change that was already clamorous. In fact, it would not even have achieved this. The expenses scandal brought to the fore a yearning to change not just the party of government but the way politics was conducted. A campaign more heavily focused on Labour's record would have associated us even more inextricably with the kind of politics people longed to do away with.

The key to the result lies in the gap between the change people wanted and the change they thought we were offering. Going into the election, voters had little clear idea of what the Conservatives stood for or what we intended to do in government (not least, incidentally, because many thought our campaign was dominated by criticism of Labour). The fact that we had not established ourselves firmly as the party of concrete change allowed the Liberal Democrats to seize their moment. At the same time, Labour's scaremongering about our intentions still resonated among too many floating voters who were not convinced we had really changed. Talking less about our plans in the months before the election, as some now argue would have been the right course, would have made this problem worse.

Neither was immigration the answer. Though important to many voters, it was one of the few issues on which we had an insurmountable lead – as, indeed, it was in 2005 – and was not among the many things on which swing voters in particular needed reassurance. Indeed, putting immigration closer to the centre of the campaign would have reminded too many of the party they rejected at the previous election.

The blend of opinion towards the Conservative Party that developed in the first year of David Cameron's leadership set the pattern for the remainder of the parliament: on the one hand, a tentative hope that the attractive new leader really did represent the prospect of a better government offering real change; on the other, suspicions about substance, concerns that the party was for the better off rather than ordinary people, and a residual fear that the change had been merely cosmetic. How, or whether, this discrepancy was resolved would determine the outcome of the election. In this respect the election was about us, not Labour. Within months of Gordon Brown's accession, voters had decided to look elsewhere; the questions in their minds was over the alternative.

I want to examine the extent to which we answered those questions. I will also give an account of my own involvement with the target seats campaign, and finally I will offer a view of David Cameron's decision to form a coalition with the Liberal Democrats.

My wife says that whatever I do, people always look for a motive – and when they find one, they think they must have missed something. My motivation for writing this book is not to condemn the campaign, still less the individuals who worked on it, whom I regard as friends and colleagues. This will not be a hatchet job or some kind of explosive insider account. I will explore how we arrived at this result – both why we did as well as we did, and why we did no better. As with *Smell the Coffee*, my study of the 2005 campaign, I want to help learn the lessons that will lead to the Conservatives once again being elected to govern with an overall majority.

Having offered my view here, I do not intend to comment any further on the 2010 election. Analysing a campaign in the light of the voters' verdict is a worthwhile exercise – an essential one, in fact, for parties that want to win. But no useful purpose is served by prolonging the debate. Once the evidence has been examined and conclusions have been reached, it is time to move on. That is not to say my interest in politics has come to an end. Far from it. The new political landscape is fascinating, and I continue to be intrigued by the relationship between parties and voters.

MAA
London, September 2010

1 / The fundamentals

IN *SMELL THE COFFEE*, my account of the 2005 general election, I concluded that the Conservatives needed to address two critical areas if they were going to start winning elections again: the Conservative brand, and the way the party targeted its campaigning resources. Tempting though it would be to carry on as before and wait for the Labour government's popularity to crumble, we could not return to office without getting these fundamentals right.

Brand is as important in politics as it is in commerce. A party's brand is not just its logo. It encompasses everything, and not just what it says about itself but how people see it: its priorities and policies; its competence, character and integrity; its people; whose side it is on.

On this score, by 2005 perceptions of the Conservative Party had changed little since it was booted out of government eight years previously to a resounding national sigh of relief. Even after these eight years in opposition, the party was thought less likely than its opponents to care about ordinary people's problems, to share their values or to do what it promised. Many voters believed the party was out of touch and cared most about the interests of the well-off. It did not seem to share people's aspirations or priorities. The Conservative Party's election campaign slogan in 2005 was "Are you thinking what we're thinking?", but the answer was "no".

Michael Howard's leadership in the eighteen months before the election had restored discipline and professionalism to the party but the damage to the Conservative brand, first inflicted during the 1990s and allowed to fester in opposition, could not be remedied so quickly. Consequently, the Conservative share of the vote rose by just 0.5 per cent at the 2005 election, and in Labour-held constituencies it actually fell. Though the party gained 33 seats, many of these owed more to Labour voters switching to the Liberal Democrats than directly to the Tories. The Conservative Party still faced deep-seated hostility among many people whose support it would need to form a government. To become electable again it would clearly need to change.

The party would also need to rethink the way it campaigned. Though broad national appeal is the most important factor in winning elections, organisation and targeting is essential to maximising the number of parliamentary seats, and in a tight race can make the difference between winning and losing. Yet the Conservative approach to targeting in 2005 was nothing short of bizarre. Under Iain Duncan Smith the party had a list of 94 target seats, aimed at achieving a realistic reduction in Labour's majority. In November 2003, after being appointed co-chairman by Michael Howard, Lord Saatchi insisted on almost doubling this list on the grounds that the leadership was "absolutely not interested in a situation where we just reduce Labour's majority. The aim is to win."

For all Lord Saatchi's heroic bluster, this decision had real consequences for the election result – it meant there were fewer Conservative MPs in the House of Commons after the 2005 election than would have been the case if the party had stuck with the list of 94. Adopting 180 "target" seats meant the available resources had to be spread so thinly that in practice there were no real targets at all. In Hampshire, for example, the Conservatives lost Romsey by 125 votes and Eastleigh by 568, having deployed time, money and people in Winchester, where a swing of more than 8 per cent was needed to overturn a Liberal Democrat majority of 7,467. With proper targeting we might have gained two new Conservative MPs for the county; in the event we gained none.

Had it not been for a renegade freelance operation that I ran along with the late Leonard Steinberg and the Midlands Industrial Council, the result would have been even worse. On the basis of business plans submitted by parliamentary candidates, we helped fund 41 Conservative campaigns in Labour-Conservative marginals, winning 24. Liberal Democrat MPs proved more tenacious and we beat only one of the nine in whose constituencies we supported the Conservative candidate. But of the 33 seats we took from Labour or the Liberal Democrats in 2005, 25 had received assistance from our fund.

My aim in publishing *Smell the Coffee* was to help ensure that these two mistakes – failure to comprehend and address the state of the Conservative brand, and the squandering of precious potential parliamentary seats through shoddy targeting – were not repeated. Others in the party also weighed in with strong views on brand and targeting but, to my puzzlement, argued that salvation lay in choosing one road or the other.

Andrew Tyrie, the MP for Chichester, concluded that "the party organisation needs to place winning the national and presidential media contest as its overriding objective". His main argument for this position was the very bold statement that "targeting of seats by the major parties at general elections is ineffective".[1] Exhibit A for this contention was the fact that at the 2001 election, the swing from Labour to the Conservatives was 2.1 percentage points lower in the top 45 Conservative targets than in the country as a whole (a 0.73 per cent swing to Labour, compared to a 1.37 per cent Labour-Conservative swing overall). But that does not demonstrate the failure of targeting per se. Tony Blair had spent the previous seven years fashioning a Labour Party carefully calibrated to appeal to exactly the kind of people who lived in the marginal constituencies where elections are won and lost, something that could not be said of the Conservative Party. Done properly, and with consistent messages, the effect of targeting is to amplify the effect of the national campaign. And if the Conservative message was offputting on television, how much more so when followed up with Shadow Cabinet visits, literature and direct mail?

Another part of Mr Tyrie's case was that Liberal Democrat targeting was unsuccessful in 2005, with their vote share falling by 1.4 per cent on average in their top 20 Conservative-held targets while it rose by 4.2 per cent overall. Again, this does not prove targeting in itself is ineffective, because we treated vulnerable Conservative seats as targets of our own. Had we not done so, we would have lost a number of seats to the Lib Dems.

The Conservative campaign in 2005 is also submitted as evidence for the pointlessness of targeting. Mr Tyrie noted that after initially aiming for an overall majority, the party diverted resources towards a narrower range of seats during the campaign with little success. But as I have argued, the party's "target" seat selection in 2005 was ludicrous. The outcome when something is done badly is hardly the best measure of whether something is worth doing at all.

In fact local campaigns have played a critical part in general elections. In the 1992 election Labour achieved a national swing from the Conservatives of 2.1 per cent. Had this relatively modest swing been uniform across the country – the same in every constituency – John Major's government would have been returned with a majority of 70. In the event, Labour made many more gains than this through their campaign on the ground and the Conservative majority was reduced to 21.

Two other contributions to this debate took directly the opposite view from Andrew Tyrie, arguing that we should ignore the party's overall brand and national level of

---

[1]   Andrew Tyrie MP, *Ten Key Points for the Future of General Election Campaigning against Labour and What These Mean for Conservative Organisation*

support, and concentrate only on local campaigning in target seats. The self-styled "Big Swingers", three new Conservative MPs who had outstripped the national swing to pull off particularly impressive results against Labour, were eager for the party to take on board the secret of their success. Grant Shapps, David Burrowes and Stewart Jackson reviewed their campaigns in Welwyn Hatfield, Enfield Southgate and Peterborough, compared notes with colleagues who had done similarly well, contrasted the findings with a random selection of MPs with more ordinary swings and listed what they concluded were the distinguishing features of the most successful campaigns.[2]

Some of their conclusions made great sense, and indeed became part of our approach in the target seats campaign – selecting candidates early, championing local issues and taking the Conservative message to parts of the constituency that had previously been written off as bad areas. But their experience of seeking election at a time when the Conservative brand was a liability rather than an asset led them to the finding that candidates did better if they actively distanced themselves from the national party. Candidates "who claimed not to present themselves as Conservatives at all gained on average a +1.67 per cent swing benefit".

The trouble with this conclusion, of course, is that it assumes a toxic national brand as a given. If some MPs did manage to be elected in 2005 by selling themselves as local champions without invoking the party nationally then I don't blame them at all. But that is hardly the ideal. The brand should be a unifying force, not something from which candidates feel they have to dissociate themselves to have a chance of winning. And how could this theory be applied more widely? Could we really have 650 Tory candidates all claiming to have nothing to do with the Conservative Party? If we were going to turn to office, we needed people to be voting for a Conservative government – not for a series of isolated candidates all playing down their association with the party and its leader.

The second contribution was from Lynton Crosby, the Australian political consultant hired by Michael Howard to mastermind the 2005 election campaign. He took the case for a targeting-based campaign to its logical extreme[3]. Declaring that "the aim is to win seats, not worry about the popular vote", he calculated that if we could persuade 185,000 voters to switch to the Conservatives from the winning party in 127 constituencies – an average of 1,457 in each constituency – we would achieve an overall majority in the House of Commons.

2   Grant Shapps, David Burrowes, Stewart Jackson, *The Big Swingers: Discovering the Common Thread*
3   Lynton Crosby, *The General Election 2005*

A successful targeting operation would usually aim to boost the number of seats gained for any given national swing, or maximise the majority from any given national lead. Lynton, though, was arguing that the Conservatives could and should aim to win a Commons majority while behind in the popular vote, and with scarcely any national swing to speak of. His extra 185,000 voters would have pushed the 2005 Conservative vote share from 33.2 to 33.9 per cent.

Though mathematically possible (a phrase that evokes a football manager in late April talking about his club's prospects of avoiding relegation) it was inconceivable to me that a party could win a general election, let alone govern effectively, on the basis of a national result only narrowly better than the Conservative score in 2005. Certainly the popular vote is not an end in itself in a Westminster election – there is no point piling up extra votes in Chelsea and Henley if you fall short in Hammersmith and Oxford. But the election analysts Professors Rallings and Thrasher had concluded that the Conservatives needed a swing of 6.9 per cent from Labour to gain the seats necessary for an overall majority. Though successful targeting could mean a majority might be achieved with a slightly smaller swing, we were never going to win with no swing at all. Lynton's plan was to try to return to government by stealth, entering Downing Street by the back door with a very thin mandate, having almost certainly come second in the popular vote for the fourth time in a row.

The final contribution that caught my attention in the debate over the party's future campaigning direction was from none other than Lord Saatchi. The opening chapter of his pamphlet was a disarming *mea culpa* entitled "How I Lost the Election", in which he listed 14 mistakes which he had made as co-chairman that had contributed to the failure to "banish the repulsive gloom of a decade of electoral unpopularity".[4]

Each mistake took the form of a dramatic self-denunciation beginning with the words "I DID NOT". I can only assume this was a somewhat tongue-in-cheek exercise; it is certainly rather mischievous. In at least one case he appears honourably to accept responsibility for other people's follies when he had in fact been the principal advocate of the folly in question.

His fifth "I DID NOT" is the most glaring example: "I DID NOT manage to expose the myth of the 'target seats', which said the national polls were irrelevant because the target seats were different." Well, that is one way of putting it. A more accurate way might have

---

4   Maurice Saatchi, *If This Is Conservatism, I Am a Conservative*, Centre for Policy Studies, June 2005

been to say that he created the myth in the first place. As I recorded in *Smell the Coffee*, it was Lord Saatchi's declaration that the party's private polling put the Conservatives ahead of Labour in 130 target seats[5], and his explanation that "the national polls are an average of everything. These target seats are seats in which by definition there is a higher propensity to vote Conservative"[6] that prompted me to begin my own research.

It is characteristically audacious of Lord Saatchi to imply that he had striven to "expose" a fallacy of which he was the chief exponent, but that doesn't matter very much in the great scheme of things. What concerns me more is that even in this new spirit of eagerness to learn from our mistakes he seemed to draw conclusions from the failure of the 2005 campaign that could result in more of the same.

"I DID NOT", he declares, "dispel the illusion of research, which said that, as immigration was the number one issue in deciding how people vote, it should be the number one topic." In this case he takes a mistaken premise and inevitably draws a wrong conclusion.

The mistaken premise is that immigration was the most important issue that would determine how people would vote. In fact it was far from being so, especially when considered in terms of the importance to "me and my family" rather than "the country as a whole", and it became even less so as the campaign progressed[7]. The wrong conclusion that follows is that research is not a reliable way of determining which issues to focus on. This is also the tenor of another self-denunciation, "I DID NOT succeed in overturning the fiction of focus groups, which can tell you what people are thinking, but not what you should be thinking." This is closer to the truth, in that people did talk a lot in focus groups about immigration, but this did not mean the issue should have dominated our campaign. At the same time this "fiction of focus groups" seems to have existed only inside the campaign – no advocate of qualitative research would claim that its purpose was to tell you what to think. The fact seems to be that the party misread the research, and Lord Saatchi has concluded on the basis of this misreading that research itself is not very useful.

Lord Saatchi later asserts, with some justice, that the post-Thatcher generation of Conservative politicians had been wrestling with a question of identity ever since Tony Blair stole their clothes. His suspicion of research leads him to state that, of the potential

5   *Smell the Coffee: A Wake-Up Call for the Conservative Party*, Michael A. Ashcroft, June 2005, p. 8
6   *Birmingham Post*, 5 October 2004
7   *Smell the Coffee*, pp. 71-4

solutions to this conundrum, "the pragmatic answer – to find out what people want and give it to them – has been tried, and failed".

It is true that voters are not inspired by soulless shopping lists of policies. Even if they like what is on the list, questions like trust, motivation and leadership also come into the equation. But even in Lord Saatchi's own terms his conclusion is wide of the mark. The problem here was not that we offered voters what they wanted and they still turned their noses up, but that what voters wanted and what the Conservatives were offering were two different things. This is not to say that people in 2005 were vehemently opposed to school discipline, more police, cleaner hospitals, lower taxes and controlled immigration. But some of these – most notably lower taxes – were unbelievable, at least from the Conservative Party as they then saw it, however desirable they might be, and policies like the Patient's Passport were actively offputting. And above all, what people wanted was an administration that understood what life was like for them and could be trusted to govern accordingly, but that we were not that administration.

There was no shortage of available advice, then, when in November 2005 David Cameron appointed me Deputy Chairman with responsibility for opinion research and marginal seats. The priorities were clear. Rebuilding the brand and running an effective targeting operation were not mutually exclusive. An improved brand was a prerequisite for winning a general election. We could not rely on a series of surgical strikes in marginal seats to deliver victory if the party's wider reputation was no better than it was in May 2005. We needed a swing of historic proportions to win an overall Commons majority. At the same time, we needed a smart target seats plan to maximise the number of parliamentary seats that swing delivered. Both elements would be supported by comprehensive and objective opinion research. I promised David the best funded and best organised target seats campaign ever seen in Britain, and that is what I set about delivering.

2 / As it was in the beginning

EVEN BEFORE the official launch of his leadership campaign in 2005 it was clear that David Cameron completely grasped the task that faced the Conservative Party. At the beginning of September he told an audience in Devon that one of the main reasons for its defeat four months earlier was that "we didn't demonstrate sufficiently to the British people that our values chimed with theirs".[8] At his campaign launch, under the slogan Change to Win, he declared that "the problem at the last election was not that people trusted the Labour Party. They didn't… The problem was that people didn't yet trust the Conservative Party, and it's we who've got to change." He wanted the party to "think, look and feel and sound like a completely different organisation".[9]

In the Blackpool Conference speech that set him on the road to victory, he warned Conservatives that "one more heave means one more defeat", and that our message had to be "relevant to people's lives today" and demonstrate that we were "comfortable with modern Britain"[10] – a theme he reiterated on his acceptance of the leadership when he said that "grumbling about modern Britain" had to stop. Above all, he wanted the Conservative Party to become "a voice for hope, optimism and change".[11]

It was sometimes argued that reform and modernisation would "upset the base", as though everyone who voted Tory during the opposition years liked the party just as it was and could not conceive of how it could be improved. It is true that Conservative voters during those years did not share the same demographic profile, or social and political attitudes, as the electorate as a whole: our 10,000-sample poll for *Smell the Coffee* found, for example, that 67 per cent of Conservative voters believed "Britain was a better country to

8   David Cameron speech, 1 September 2005
9   David Cameron speech at leadership campaign launch, 29 September 2005
10   David Cameron speech to the Conservative Party Conference, Blackpool, 4 October 2005
11   David Cameron leadership acceptance speech, 6 December 2005

live in 20 or 30 years ago", compared to 55 per cent of the population as a whole and only 36 per cent of 18-24-year-olds.[12]

But that is not to say that they opposed the new direction the party was taking. In January 2007 I commissioned a poll of 2005 Conservative voters, with encouraging results.[13] Just over a year into David Cameron's leadership, more than two thirds of those who had voted Conservative at the last election said the party had "changed for the better" since 2005, with only 6 per cent thinking it had changed for the worse (although this figure was nearly twice as high – 11 per cent – among readers of the *Daily Mail* and the *Daily Express*). Nearly three quarters (74 per cent) said the party was going forwards rather than backwards, and 67 per cent believed it was on course to win the next general election.

More than half (51 per cent) agreed that "David Cameron is the best leader the Conservatives have had in a long time", and an overwhelming 93 per cent agreed that "David Cameron has been right to recognise the Conservative Party has to change if it is to attract enough voters to win the next general election". Nearly three quarters (74 per cent) said they "support the changes David Cameron is making because it makes it more likely that the Conservatives will win the next general election"; only 23 per cent said they "might support another party in the future because David Cameron has abandoned too many traditional Conservative policies".

Though many were attached to traditional policy positions (89 per cent wanted the party to "speak out more strongly against the growing influence of the EU" and 91 per cent thought we should "pledge to crack down on immigration") there was also support for Cameron initiatives. Nearly two thirds (65 per cent) thought we would have a better chance of winning the next election if we made the Conservative Party "more representative of the country, in particular by having more women and people from ethnic minorities standing as Conservative candidates than in past elections"; 89 per cent supported "agreeing openly with the government when it is right and avoiding 'yah-boo' politics and name-calling"; 91 per cent agreed that we should "make clear that economic stability, not tax cuts, comes first"; and 86 per cent supported giving "a high priority to policies for addressing climate change, boosting the Conservative Party's credentials as a party genuinely committed to protecting the environment".

12   12-20 January 2005, sample 10,007, conducted by Populus
13   23-28 January 2007, sample 1,000, telephone and online, conducted by Populus

It is perhaps not as surprising as it should be that Tory voters were more open to change, and saw more clearly what we would need to do to return to government, than some in the Conservative parliamentary party. The most notable example is the Cornerstone Group – in many ways an admirable enterprise whose founders share strong convictions and a willingness to advocate what they would be the first to acknowledge are unfashionable points of view. (If I seem to pick on them unduly here it is only to illustrate the important point that the need for the party to modernise, self-evident to voters, was far from being so for some Conservative MPs.)

In September 2005 the group published a pamphlet[14] calling for Conservatives to "return to the wellspring of our beliefs, our founding principles", arguing that if we communicate a philosophy that is distinctively conservative "we will be recast, our electoral credibility restored". Its introduction, by John Hayes, is a lament for a lost country:

> Most people believe that the quality of life in Britain is declining, and they are right. The symptoms of malaise are everywhere: democratic government (not just a particular government) is no longer trusted by the people it claims to represent. Family breakdown is commonplace and consequently our towns and cities are blighted by despair and bereft of community. Public services routinely fail the people who pay for them, work in them, and use them, yet taxes continue to go up. Our judicial system is ineffective at dealing adequately with criminals, whilst many people live in constant fear of crime as public order evaporates. Our towns and cities are increasingly bland and brutal – with soulless shopping malls, identikit housing estates and all the yobbish symbols of social decay.[15]

He goes on to discuss the breakdown of civil society with reference to Kipling, de Tocqueville and Mill, noting the observation of Peter Hitchens that "today's radicals" – the liberal elite that Mr Hayes accuses as the architects of our national decline – "loathe the United Kingdom". But from his description it is clear that Mr Hayes is none too fond of it

14   *Being Conservative: A Cornerstone of Policies to Revive Tory Britain*, Cornerstone Group, September 2005, p. 9

15   Ibid. p. 3

himself. His view – sincerely held and movingly articulated – is that Britain has gone to the dogs. Reading his meditation there can be no doubt that John Hayes loves his country; he just doesn't seem to like it very much.

The pamphlet puts forward a number of policies, but whatever their merits it is this distaste for and discomfort in contemporary Britain that speaks loudest, and which would speak loudest about a party that adopted the same tone. People will not want to vote for a group of people that seems to disapprove of the way they live, or entrust it with government of a country it does not seem to like or understand. This is the danger of the "grumbling about modern Britain" that David Cameron proscribed.

In other publications the group reveals further misunderstandings of why we lost the election and what we should do to ensure that it doesn't keep happening. In a pamphlet in July 2005 the group's chairman, Edward Leigh, reflected on our third consecutive defeat and concluded that we failed to talk enough about Europe, to offer large enough tax cuts or to campaign strongly enough on the Patient's Passport (the policy of contributing to the cost of private operations)[16]. He continued this theme in an article in the *House Magazine* in February 2007, asking: "Was not the real reason [we lost the election] that we were not very skilled or personable enough in explaining our ideas?"[17]

No, that was not the real reason: voters did not reject us because they failed to grasp the wonders we had in store for them. The Patient's Passport policy was not seen as an exciting way to give ordinary people faster access to top quality healthcare, but a signal that we were abandoning the NHS to its inadequacies and providing an escape route for the better off. And campaigning more vigorously on the issues Mr Leigh suggested would have brought its own problems. Independence from Europe was not a priority for most people – or many people at all – at the last election. Lower taxes were not a winning theme in 2005 because they were not believable without the threat of Tory cuts. The combination of Europe, tax and the Patient's Passport would have reinforced even further the impression of a party that was out of touch with ordinary people's concerns and which cared most about the privileged few (which is, incidentally, the real reason we lost).

---

16   *The Strange Desertion of Tory England: The Conservative Alternative to The Liberal Orthodoxy*, Cornerstone Group, July 2005, pp. 11-12

17   'Triangulation or Strangulation?', *The House Magazine*, February 2007, p. 14

Mr Leigh is not alone in advocating bolder tax policies but the argument is based on a misunderstanding about why the tax promise we did make had little effect. We are told, he writes, "that focus groups don't believe us if we promise tax cuts. We are told that focus groups are cynical about politicians, thinking us self-serving and unreliable. One way forward would be to emphasise our plans to lift lower paid workers out of tax altogether by raising thresholds."[18] Raising thresholds may well be a good idea, but there is no reason to suppose this policy would have drawn any more Conservative votes than the tax promises we did make. It is true that people didn't believe us if we promised tax cuts. But that doesn't mean we should have promised to raise thresholds instead – it means that if we promised to raise thresholds they wouldn't have believed that either. At best, it would have prompted them to wonder straight away what we were planning to take away from them to make up for it. However attractive the policy may have been in principle, too many people thought the appropriate response to a Tory tax promise was to start counting the spoons.

IN DECEMBER 2005 I presented to David Cameron the results of our initial research, which was carried out during the leadership election to serve as a benchmark from which to work. I concluded with a slide headed "What they must be saying by 2009", a list of statements that people should feel to be true of the Conservative Party for us to be in a position to win the next general election. Nothing in the list was very controversial; the hard part was accepting that people did not think these things already, and David had done that long ago.

Our findings had been as grim as might have been expected for a party that had just been rejected by the country at a third consecutive general election. A number of themes recurred. Most frequent was the idea that the Conservative Party represented the better off and was not really interested in ordinary people. The charge that we were out of touch, which had dogged the party since midway through the Major administration, persisted: we seemed inflexible, failing to keep up with the modern world. Despite having been out of government for so long we still seemed tired. We were thought less likely than our opponents to care about ordinary people's problems, and were rated more highly than Labour on only one policy issue: immigration. While most people were dissatisfied with the Labour government, most also preferred it to a Conservative one. The spirited leadership contest then taking place suggested some signs of life but there was no reason to see this particular election as a defining moment for the party, given that the winning David would be its fifth leader in eight years. The best that could be said for the Conservative Party was that it seemed patriotic – although, for many, in an old-fashioned way that associated it with the past and an outdated vision of Britain as it used to be.

What they must be saying by 2009

- "The Conservatives want the same things for Britain that I want"

- "The Conservatives understand people like me"

- "The Conservatives would govern in the interests of everyone"

- "David Cameron has the qualities needed to be prime minister"

- "The Conservative Party is very different today from when it was kicked out in 1997"

- "The Conservatives are now a modern party and understand Britain as it is today"

- "The Conservatives have good ideas to improve life in Britain and would deliver them if elected"

- "The Conservatives know what they stand for and have clear ideas for improving life in Britain"

- "I can trust the Conservatives to improve public services like the NHS"

Once elected, Mr Cameron set about the business of transforming the party with relish. His early activity tackled a wide range of what had come to be regarded as un-Tory themes. On 7 December 2005, the day after his triumph, he launched the Social Justice policy group, to be chaired by Iain Duncan Smith, which would look at the causes and consequences of poverty in Britain, family policy and childcare, treatment and rehabilitation for young people affected by drugs and alcohol, care of the elderly and disabled, the voluntary sector, social enterprise and community action. Social justice was one of six big challenges facing Britain that Mr Cameron had set out in his victory speech, the others being globalisation and global poverty, the quality of life, national and international security, economic competitiveness, and public service improvement. A policy commission was established to look at each one, staffed by eminent individuals, many from outside politics, who were asked to report their findings in eighteen months.

The following week Mr Cameron really began to ruffle some party feathers when he set out his plans to revamp the selection process for prospective Conservative MPs[19]. He announced that target and Conservative-held seats would from now on be expected to choose from a priority list of "our best and brightest candidates", half of whom would be women, and which would include "a significant proportion of people with disabilities, and from black and minority ethnic communities". Non-party members would also be able to take part in the selection of candidates through local community stakeholder panels, or in primary elections open to all registered voters in a constituency. (The following August the rules were revised to compel target seats to choose from a final shortlist of four candidates, at least two of whom had to be women.)

In his first few months Mr Cameron put the environment at the centre of his policy agenda, urging people to Vote Blue, Go Green in the local government elections, visiting a Norwegian glacier to highlight his concern over climate change, and calling for the government to introduce a Climate Change Bill alongside Friends of the Earth. He emphasised his commitment to corporate responsibility, regretting that the Conservatives had been "painted into a corner" as the party of "unbridled capitalism"[20] and declaring, "when I see businesses behaving irresponsibly I'm going to speak out", even going as far as naming companies that he felt had transgressed, including BHS and WH Smith.

When it came to transforming public opinion, progress was tough. The Conservative Party enjoyed a small initial boost in voting intention polls, but changes in underlying perceptions were mixed. While people liked the look of the charismatic new leader, it was not yet clear to what extent the party behind him had really changed, or was likely to change. The apparent dichotomy between David Cameron and the party they were familiar with made people even more confused about what the party really stood for.

By the middle of 2006 some real progress had been made. For the first time in our focus group research people began to mention hope and optimism in association with the Conservative Party. This was usually because the party looked more hopeful and optimistic

19   David Cameron speech, 12 December 2005
20   David Cameron speech to Business in the Community, 9 May 2006

about its own prospects than had been the case for some time, but voters, too, sensed that they might at last be offered a credible alternative. These qualities were also evident in David Cameron's character, and he seemed approachable and inclusive. People had also noticed – usually with approval, but not always – the Conservatives' recent focus on the environment, as embodied in the leader's habit of cycling to work and his Norwegian glacier trip.

The negatives – especially the Tories' association with the past and the posh – were still very much present. They were now accompanied by an accusation that the party seemed to spend much of its energy jumping on bandwagons. With a new leader who did not fit the traditional Conservative mould, the party seemed confused about what it stood for, forcing it to latch onto newsworthy issues to win publicity rather than act out of principle and conviction.

Concern about how deep change was really going in the Conservative Party was a recurring theme in the early months after Mr Cameron became leader. If, as most thought, a real transformation had yet to happen, was this simply because change would take time or because the only difference would be presentational and real change was not on the agenda? Would he manage to reshape his party, or was he simply the attractive new face of the same old Tories, who would take Britain back to the bad old days if they had the chance?

Voters did not doubt, though, that David Cameron was a different kind of Conservative leader. In the early months of his leadership it was often said that he seemed uncannily similar to Tony Blair at the same stage: a family man, seemingly in touch with modern Britain and, perhaps above all, well presented. While such a comparison would seem to augur well in electoral terms, to many who felt disappointed with Mr Blair, Mr Cameron looked all too familiar. They feared being let down a second time. Even so, people's views were positive. He was regarded as likeable and dynamic, happy rather than sad, optimistic rather than pessimistic, personally trustworthy, approachable, yet a serious character. Most could easily see him as Prime Minister, whether they yet welcomed the prospect or not.

Mr Cameron's wealthy background was widely known.[21] For most people, though, this was not a particular barrier; if he was privileged, then so (in their view) were most MPs.

---

21   But not universally so. When one East Midlands focus group participant remarked that Mr Cameron had been to school at Eton, another chipped in: "So did my wife, and it didn't do her any harm." The puzzled silence that followed was eventually broken when someone said: "Not Long Eaton, you plonker."

While he was far from sharing the everyday experience of most people in Britain, at least with a young family he seemed to live as normal a life as was possible for a politician.

Further evidence that Mr Cameron had some understanding of life beyond politics came from the minor rumpus over whether he had ever used recreational drugs. The journalist Andrew Rawnsley put the question to him during the leadership campaign at an *Observer*-sponsored event at the 2005 party conference. Voters who recalled the controversy in his first year as leader thought he handled it well. Most seemed to misremember the episode as an admission that he had indeed used illegal drugs, but far from reflecting badly on him it showed that he was normal and honest.

Those who were well disposed towards Mr Cameron still had questions. Not being a distinctively new kind of politician (but instead a traditional politician of above average attractiveness), Mr Cameron was still seen as someone out to win votes by appealing to as wide an audience as possible, and therefore liable to tell people what they wanted to hear. Combined with his inevitable lack of a track record, and the fact that few had heard him talk about specific policies beyond the environment, many continued to wonder about substance: where he stood on real issues, and whether he would have the strength to deliver what he promised.

This uncertainty as to what the Cameron Conservatives stood for provided some insulation against early Labour charges that the new leader was dangerously right wing. However, it did make him more vulnerable to another Labour attack, that of "flip-flopping". Labour made this theme the subject of a party political broadcast entitled *Dave the Chameleon*, aired during the 2006 local election campaign.

Set to the tune of Culture Club's "Karma Chameleon", with its repeated line "I'm a man without conviction", the film follows the progress of an animated blue chameleon from school (straw boater, striped tie) into politics working for the "blue party" (where he is pictured with John Major and Norman Lamont) and then into public relations (stretch limousine, champagne), where the narrator tells us that he "learned to change into any colour he pleased". Dave the Chameleon "suddenly realised that telling everyone what the Conservatives really stood for was never going make them – or more importantly, him – popular… Dave the Chameleon changed into every colour of the rainbow as he told everyone what he thought they wanted to hear, but underneath it all he was still true blue through and through". The second instalment of the broadcast reprises the theme, refers to Dave the Chameleon's role in Black Wednesday and the drafting of the 2005 Conservative election manifesto, and lists a series of policy areas, including the Patient's Passport and university tuition fees, in which he has supposedly changed his position.

People were largely prepared to defend these reversals as evidence that he was listening; it would be ridiculous to cling to an outdated position or a wrong and unpopular policy. For some, the U-turns were evidence of cynicism and unreliability, particularly since some of them seemed to have happened in the space of less than a year. For people on both sides of this argument, though, the question of substance would need to be answered. Even those prepared to give Mr Cameron time to set out his policy stall, and those who took an understanding view of his apparent U-turns, wanted to see further evidence of his qualities as a leader and his – and the party's – values and direction.

By the end of 2006 this problem had become more serious. Though the Conservatives had enjoyed a narrow but regular poll lead for most of the year, the sceptically positive attitude and sense of change that had characterised voters' attitudes in the early months of David Cameron's leadership had receded. The themes of hope, optimism and charisma were more muted. The party seemed once again to be negative and reactive in its pronouncements, and the lack of perceived activity and momentum led people to question whether change was authentic, or even whether it was happening at all. People fell back on the old labels that had dominated perceptions of the Conservative brand a year earlier, and for years before that.

This uneven pattern of opinion towards the Conservative Party in David Cameron's first year as leader was the template for what followed. Over this time he had made his mark as a different kind of Conservative leader, stirred new interest in the party, won important local government elections, launched a serious long-term policy review, and steered the party to its first consistent poll lead for thirteen years. But the year had shown just how hard it would be to substitute in the public mind a changed, modern, substantial and authentic party for the one they had grown used to. It had reinforced the need for us to be clear about our own agenda, not just criticise our opponents. And it demonstrated the importance of permanent momentum – in the absence of a constant stream of new evidence, people quickly reverted to their old, dangerous stereotypes.

3 / **A snapshot of the opposition**

IN THE MIDDLE OF 2007, a few weeks before Gordon Brown assumed the premiership, swing voters with a good word to say about the Labour government were few and far between.

Whereas in our earlier research we had found floating voters still willing to defend Labour, by the spring of 2007 they were becoming increasingly scarce. The party seemed to be weary after its long decade in office. It had also come to be seen as untrustworthy, with many feeling that it had not delivered on the promises it had made over the previous decade; lingering anger at the events leading up to the war in Iraq had also contributed to this view. Britain's role in the war had also given many the impression that the government was weak, simply doing the bidding of President Bush and the US administration.[22]

The government had become associated with expensive projects of little benefit to most people, and seemed to be obsessed with celebrity and wealth. In the eyes of voters it had failed to control crime and, most damningly, there was a very widespread view that Labour's policies helped those who did nothing to help themselves, but increasingly ignored those who tried to do the right thing. This in turn contributed to an impression that the party was losing touch with ordinary, hard working people. The Labour Party seemed divided, and Labour politicians appeared to be arrogant and out for themselves rather than the good of the country. People were much less likely to see the party as competent and capable than had been the case at the end of 2005, and to think it shared their values.

Labour retained some advantages over the Tories. With Mr Blair still in place the party still had the edge on strong, charismatic leadership. There was also a view that Labour's

---

22   This theme had also been prominent in the 2005 general election campaign, though at this stage many floating voters still had a more forgiving attitude to Mr Blair. See *Smell the Coffee*, Chapter 3.

basic motivation was to be on the side of ordinary people (even if this was not necessarily reflected in the current crop of its leading politicians). Tax credits were often cited as an example of this principle in practice. Even on this score, though, Labour's credentials were suffering. The unfair penalising of those whose tax credits had mistakenly been overpaid, combined with the perceived lack of delivery on public services and the apparent indulgence of welfare scroungers at the expense of the industrious, were beginning to undermine the party's central claim to be working for the many not the few.

Voting intention polls had shifted accordingly. The Conservatives did not take the lead as soon as David Cameron was elected. Though the Conservative share rose, the parties were in fact neck and neck for the first few months of 2006.

The deadlock was broken at the end of April 2006 when the government suffered what some in the media called a "triple whammy" of disasters in the space of 24 hours. Most seriously, it was revealed that 1,023 foreign prisoners had been released from British jails without being considered for deportation. Patricia Hewitt, the Health Secretary, was jeered as she addressed the annual conference of the Royal College of Nursing. Less seriously in political terms, but unhelpfully on top of everything else, details emerged of a relationship between John Prescott, the Deputy Prime Minister, and his diary secretary.

This trinity of fiascos was far from an ideal backdrop to Labour's campaign for the local elections on 4 May, which the Conservatives won convincingly with a 39 per cent share of the vote to Labour's 26 per cent. Labour lost 17 councils and 320 councillors.[23] In the year that followed the Conservatives held a monthly average poll lead of between 4 and 8 per cent.

Gordon Brown, then, would inherit a party that had lost trust, was widely thought not to have delivered on its promises, and whose preoccupation with its own leadership had given voters an impression of division and self-indulgence. Consequently, Labour had trailed in nearly every published poll for a year. What did voters make of the man who would face the job of reversing the decline?

Although Mr Brown had been a central figure on the political stage for well over a decade, in the months before he entered Number 10 people did not feel they knew him very well at all. Though known to be an architect of New Labour, he was seen as being more left wing than Tony Blair and Sir Menzies Campbell, and most Labour voters themselves. To some, the heated delivery of his speeches (and evidently fervent desire to be Prime Minister) conveyed passion; to others, his apparent fondness for lists of numbers suggested he was rather cold. Mr Brown compared favourably to most politicians when it came to being honest and straightforward, and although he was regarded as dull and dour, this was thought to be no bad thing in the guardian of the nation's finances.

Two years before the recession, Gordon Brown's reputation as Chancellor was very strong. Voters gave him a good deal of the credit for economic stability and higher investment in public services. But he was not without criticism – in particular, voters thought much of the extra spending had been wasted, for which the Chancellor had to take much of the blame. Though he may well have been the "roadblock to reform" that the Conservatives claimed, this was also a relief – as Chancellor he was in a position to say what was practical and affordable, and if in so doing he had managed to put a stop to dubious Blairite schemes then this was all to the good.

For many people, the key to predicting Mr Brown's performance at Number 10 was not whether he had been a good Chancellor, but whether being a good Chancellor was in itself an indicator of ability to do the top job. To put it another way, were the personal characteristics that suited him to the Treasury the qualities that people wanted to see in a Prime Minister? As one focus group participant put it: "Gordon Brown could do a fantastic job as Prime Minister. Or it might freak him out and he'd go completely to pieces."

A YouGov poll for the *Daily Telegraph* in September 2006[24] further explored views of his character by offering respondents pairs of words and phrases and asking which of the two applied most to Mr Brown. He was considered *effective* (rather than ineffective), *competent*, *decisive* and *psychologically strong*, but the good news ended there: he was also *uncaring, not likeable as a person, not able to unite the nation, morose and introverted*, and someone who *cannot be trusted, bears grudges* and *does not work well with others*.

In a Populus poll[25] at the end of 2006, only a third of voters agreed that *Gordon Brown has been a good Chancellor and I think he will be a good Prime Minister*. A quarter thought *Gordon Brown has been a good Chancellor but I don't think he will be a good Prime Minister*. Another quarter thought that neither had he been a good Chancellor, nor would he be a good Prime Minister. So overall, while well over half agreed he had been a good Chancellor, only two fifths expected him to perform well at Number 10.

24   YouGov/*Daily Telegraph* poll, 19-22 September 2006, sample 1,733
25   Populus poll for *The Times*, 8-10 December 2006, sample 1,513

This gulf between perceptions of Mr Brown's competence as Chancellor and his aptitude for the premiership were largely due to doubts about his personality. The characteristics that people felt had made Mr Blair effective – being likeable, in touch, flexible, persuasive – were thought to be lacking, to a certain extent, in his likely successor. In theory, many people thought the absence of charm was an encouraging sign, heralding a new era of style over substance and a repudiation of the obsession with presentation that had always characterised New Labour. At the same time, good presentation was recognised as an important part of modern politics, and on this score he paled in comparison to the incumbent. However weary of Mr Blair people had become, many saw his charm and plausibility as indispensable qualities for a Prime Minister.

Voters noticed Mr Brown's impatience with interviewers, and his refusal (even more marked than with most politicians) to answer questions that did not take his fancy. His rather dishevelled appearance was also a distraction. While men often found his speech-making style strong and convincing, women tended to find it aggressive and hectoring.

While the differences in style with Mr Blair were clear, the fact that he had been working with Mr Blair since Opposition and his record as a driving force behind New Labour meant that few expected radical changes in policy. In a YouGov poll in September 2006[26] only 36 per cent agreed that *as Prime Minister, Gordon Brown will take the government in a quite different direction from the one it is now going in*. Forty-one per cent were more inclined to think that with Gordon Brown as Prime Minister *it will be pretty much business as usual*. Nearly a quarter (23 per cent) didn't know which of these was the more likely.

So in the absence of any significant change in policy, in the view of most voters a year before the handover, the principal difference between the Blair and Brown administrations would be one of style. Mr Brown was experienced, a force for stability in the economy and the government, relatively unspun, a successful Chancellor on the side of ordinary people. His less polished approach would, for many, constitute a refreshing change. But the downside, his lack of charisma and persuasiveness, was by no means trivial. It was perhaps taken as read that a Prime Minister should be capable, substantial and experienced. But a Prime Minister needed something else as well – something that many feared Mr Brown did not have.

26 YouGov/*Daily Telegraph* poll, 6-7 September 2006, sample 1,504

A year on, his reputation as Chancellor remained strong. However, there was some debate over the extent to which Mr Brown deserved the credit for Britain's economic performance. People were also more ready to say that Mr Brown had been good for the economy as a whole than thought he had helped them personally, though some associated him with tax credits from which they had benefited. He was widely blamed for tax increases. While all Chancellors are believed to raise taxes, many felt Mr Brown had done so more than most, and had tried to do it by stealth. The 2007 Budget, in which he cut the basic rate of tax to 20p but scrapped the 10p rate altogether, leaving the lowest earners worse off, helped to reinforce that view.

Among swing voters there was very little enthusiasm for the idea of Mr Brown as Prime Minister, an event which most now regarded as inevitable. Though expectations were not high, only a few were actually hostile to the thought; the more common reaction was a mixture of apprehension and resignation. Despite what the media described as a "charm offensive", the gap between the personal qualities people saw in Mr Brown and those they wanted in a Prime Minister remained wide. People still thought he lacked the required empathetic qualities, and did not expect him to change once he entered Number 10.

These things help to explain why the March 2007 YouGov poll found only a fifth saying they were looking forward to him becoming Prime Minister, with more than half saying they were not. Only 3 per cent were *greatly looking forward to it*; the biggest group, 36 per cent, were *not looking forward to it at all*.

One issue that might have posed a problem for Mr Brown in theory but never really materialised in practice was his Scottishness. In a YouGov poll for the *Sun*[27] in September 2006 a majority (53 per cent) disagreed with the statement *Gordon Brown is a Scot who doesn't understand the English*. In January 2007, Populus[28] asked a detailed question on the issue and found 66 per cent saying *it doesn't matter if the Prime Minister represents a Scottish seat*, with only 26 per cent saying it would be wrong because Scotland has its own parliament.

On the question of what Mr Brown might actually *do* as Prime Minister, most voters were at a loss. People assumed that he had not set out clear plans either because to do so would appear complacent before his appointment was confirmed, or because nothing much

27   YouGov/*Sun* poll, 13-14 September 2006, sample 1,519

28   Populus/*Times* poll, 2-4 February 2007, sample 1,509

was going to change and he had nothing distinctive to say. Voters' expectation of a Brown premiership was that the government would continue on its current (downward) course, except with higher taxes. Few expected tangible improvements. This was summed up by an ICM poll in the *Guardian*[29] in which voters were asked: *Do you think Gordon Brown would represent a fresh start for the government, or would he represent more of the same?* Only 22 per cent said he would represent *a fresh start*, with 71 per cent disagreeing.

The lack of clarity about Mr Brown's plans, the uncertainty about what if any change he was offering, and the concerns about his aptitude to be Prime Minister reinforced a very strong feeling among voters that the Labour Party should hold a leadership election, not let him take the job unchallenged. The same ICM poll found 78 per cent of voters thinking Labour should *have a leadership contest where a number of people in government stand, to give a choice*, with only 16 per cent wanting to see Labour *rally around one candidate such as Gordon Brown, and elect him as leader unopposed.* Even Labour voters preferred a leadership contest by 72 per cent to 24 per cent.

Despite people's resentment at the idea of a leader being imposed on them, and a wish to see what alternatives, if any, were available, very few people in our groups could think of a viable alternative candidate. The desire for an alternative candidate in theory but the inability to think of one in practice was echoed in the polls. Populus[30] found more than half of voters agreeing that Labour would be better of choosing one of its *rising stars who is younger and newer but less experienced and largely unknown* in preference to Gordon Brown. Labour voters were the only group to prefer Gordon Brown in this scenario, by 55 per cent to 42 per cent.

The purpose of the Populus question was to shed light on the prospects of David Miliband, then Environment Secretary, who was widely believed to be considering standing. Polls about party leadership candidates are usually little more than a measure of name recognition (indeed David Cameron famously scored only 2 per cent in such a survey[31] six months before being elected leader of the Conservative Party; Ken Clarke, David Davis, Malcolm Rifkind, John Redwood and Liam Fox all scored higher). Even so, the lack of public awareness of any serious alternative to Mr Brown was striking.

29   ICM/*Guardian* poll, 20-22 April 2007, sample 1,005

30   Populus/*Times* poll, 2-4 March 2007, sample 1,509

31   Populus/*Times* poll, 3-5 June 2005, sample 1,513

In a YouGov poll in April 2007,[32] Mr Brown led with only 22 per cent, with Mr Miliband on just 16 per cent, and Charles Clarke, John McDonnell and Michael Meacher each in single figures. Forty-nine per cent said *Don't know*.

For many people, a leadership election would serve a purpose beyond that of simply conferring some degree of democratic legitimacy on the succession: it would force Mr Brown to set out his policies and priorities, explain his vision, reassure people that he did in fact have the personal qualities they wanted to see in a Prime Minister.

For some, the change of Prime Minister without so much as a contest within his party made an immediate general election imperative, but this was by no means a universal view. Yes, an uncontested succession would mean we had a Prime Minister whom nobody had elected. But many felt that once he was there they would need a chance to see him in action for a while before being asked to decide whether or not he should continue.

While few expected life to improve with Gordon Brown as Prime Minister, few expected disasters. Most people contemplated the forthcoming transfer of power (if they did so at all) with neither excitement nor dread. If they had any expectation of what a Brown premiership would hold, it was more of the same. Mr Brown would be a less colourful character than we had become used to at Number 10, but his long years as the second most powerful figure in the government meant that few had any reason to expect real changes in policy. Mr Brown would be, as one focus group participant put it, "Blair without the smile".

If this sounds like a fairly benign climate of opinion for an incoming Prime Minister, in practice it meant that the challenge awaiting Mr Brown on his accession was similar to that which had faced David Cameron eighteen months previously. Like Mr Cameron, he had to rehabilitate his party. Mr Brown's mission on this front was the more straightforward. Certainly Labour had come to be seen as tired, out of touch, untrustworthy and weak, but this is not surprising given the inevitable public weariness with a government that had been in office for ten years. In Mr Brown's favour was a widespread public feeling that however hopeless the current administration, the Labour Party's heart was still in the right place and it was essentially on the side of ordinary people. Despite its troubles, Labour did not face the ingrained antipathy that beleaguered the Conservatives.

But the Tories had what Labour lacked – a new, charismatic leader who offered the promise of change. To be sure, the public had its reservations as to whether Mr Cameron would turn out to be the real deal. But while his task was to reshape the Conservative Party in his own image, Mr Brown had to restore Labour's brand without any of Mr Cameron's advantages. To refresh the reputation of a tired government, and set it on a path to a fourth election victory, would be hard enough for a leader with new ideas and wide personal appeal. Instead the task fell to a man who had been a member of the tired government since its inception, whom the public found less personally engaging than both his opponent and his predecessor, and who, as far as voters were concerned, had either failed or chosen not to set out a clear new agenda.

4 / Events

GORDON BROWN and David Cameron, then, both found themselves with the task of shifting public opinion towards their respective parties. This was not a job that could be carried out in isolation. Proactive initiatives can sometimes command attention but they are the exception: most of what politicians do is seen through the prism of events. Especially in opposition, politicians have to react to the news far more often than they get the chance to create it. How they do so – the judgments they make, the positions they adopt, the tone and manner of their responses – do more to define their parties' brands in the voters' minds than set-piece launches or rallies or speeches, let alone posters or party political broadcasts.

Three events, or sets of events, dominated Gordon Brown's tenure as Prime Minister: the cancelled autumn election of 2007, the economic crisis that gathered pace from the run on Northern Rock, and the anger over MPs' expenses and allowances that exploded into rage in the spring of 2009. These events, and the way the parties handled them, were central to the choice that voters saw before them when the general election finally arrived.

The Brown bounce and its end

From the end of 2005 to the month before the handover, a number of pollsters asked how people would vote if Gordon Brown were Labour leader instead of Tony Blair. This exercise nearly always produced a higher Conservative lead than the standard voting intention question, which usually asks which party respondents would vote for if the election were tomorrow, without mentioning leaders. The revised question was asked 27 times between December 2005 and May 2007. It never once produced a hypothetical lead for Mr Brown, and on all but four occasions his installation had the effect of increasing the Conservative margin.

There were several good reasons to treat these polls with scepticism. For one thing, since most people sensibly do not follow politics or politicians very closely, it is hard for them to predict accurately how they will react to something like a change of Prime Minister: Mr Brown might do better or worse than they expected, or introduce unexpected new policies that they would greet with horror or delight. On a more technical point, the questions mentioning Mr Brown also named the other party leaders for balance. The higher Conservative leads could therefore have owed as much to the mention of David Cameron as to any depressant effect of Gordon Brown. (Indeed, Populus found this to be the case in their poll for *The Times* in July 2006: asking each third of the sample a different version of the voting intention question, their standard wording produced a 2-point Conservative lead; naming the then current leaders – Blair, Cameron and Campbell – produced a 7-point lead; and naming Brown, Cameron and Campbell a 9-point lead.)

Nevertheless, these points were confined to bloggers like Anthony Wells on UK Polling Report[33] and Mike Smithson on Political Betting,[34] and a few columnists like Tim Hames (who gave it as his view that one such poll "could not be more obviously rogue if it came in a bag marked 'swag'").[35] The idea that polls proved Labour would become less popular under Mr Brown became an important part of the media narrative in the months leading up to the handover. Expectations were lowered to a degree that made the subsequent turnaround seem all the more dramatic.

From the moment of his arrival at Number 10, Mr Brown was determined to project an aura of change. He used the word eight times in the short speech he gave outside his new front door on his return from Buckingham Palace, six of them in a single sentence:

> As I have travelled around the country, and as I have listened I have learnt from the British people – and as Prime Minister I will continue to listen and learn from the British people – I have heard the need for change, change in our NHS, change in our schools, change with affordable housing, change to build trust in government, change to protect and extend the British way of life … And now, let the work of change begin.[36]

---

33   'Putting the latest ICM in proportion', ukpollingreport.co.uk, 20 February 2007
34   'Has this been made to be as damaging as possible?', politicalbetting.com, 20 February 2007
35   'That's not a morbid saddo, that's a Labour MP', *The Times*, 26 February 2007
36   Gordon Brown statement, 27 June 2007

Mr Brown did not have to spend the first few weeks in office generating his own news. He was immediately faced with flooding, a terrorist attack at Glasgow Airport and an outbreak of foot and mouth disease that obliged him to abandon his holiday in Dorset after just four hours.

Voters seemed impressed. Labour took the lead in the average of published polls for the first time since March 2006, and there was wide approval for the new Prime Minister's performance. ICM found 82 per cent thinking Mr Brown had handled the foot and mouth crisis *quite well* or *very well*,[37] Populus found 62 per cent thinking he was *sincerely determined to get to grips with the problems facing this country*,[38] and YouGov found nearly two thirds (65 per cent) saying Mr Brown was doing *well* as Prime Minister; 86 per cent thought he was doing *about the same* as they expected (50 per cent) or *better* (36 per cent). Only 5 per cent thought he was doing *worse*.[39]

On the question of whether he represented the substantive change that he was at such pains to promise, the picture was more mixed. In their July poll Populus found majorities disagreeing that Mr Brown had *brought a real sense of renewal to the Labour government* (by 60 per cent to 40 per cent) and that *he represents significant change for the better from how things were under Tony Blair* (by 57 per cent to 43 per cent).[40]

ICM found only 38 per cent agreeing that *Labour under Gordon Brown feels like a new government with a new direction*, with 55 per cent preferring the alternative statement *Labour under Gordon Brown feels like a change of faces, and that's about it*.[41] In a separate ICM poll a week later, people agreed by a 14-point margin (49 per cent to 35 per cent) that Mr Brown represented a real change from Mr Blair in terms of his *personal leadership style*, but by only 7 points (43 per cent to 36 per cent) that he represented a real change in terms of his *policy direction*.[42]

In September, YouGov found that although a majority felt that Mr Brown *does seem to represent a fresh start* (53 per cent), with the same proportion agreeing that *there are fewer*

37   ICM/*Sunday Mirror* poll, 8-9 August 2007, sample 1,007

38   Populus/*Times* poll, 6-8 July 2007, sample 1,002

39   YouGov/*Sunday Times* poll, 9-10 August 2007, sample 1,966

40   Populus/*Times* poll, 6-8 July 2007, sample 1,002

41   ICM/*News of the World* poll, 11-13 July 2007, sample 1,003

42   ICM/*Guardian* poll, 20-22 July 2007, sample 1,005

gimmicks and less "spin" under Gordon Brown than there used to be under Tony Blair, only just over a third (35 per cent) thought the government had *a clear sense of direction* (35 per cent); more than half (51 per cent) thought *it is hard to know what the government and the Labour party stand for at the moment*.[43]

This combination of positive overall ratings and lukewarm responses on more concrete issues was not necessarily a contradiction. For one thing, as we had found in our research before the handover, most people had not expected much of a change, except in terms of personality. Indeed, immediately after Mr Brown assumed office YouGov asked why people thought the new Prime Minister spoke so frequently about the need for change; the most popular explanation was that *he wants to distance himself as far as he can from Tony Blair and his government* (47 per cent). Only 17 per cent thought is was *because he wants his government to have both new policies and a new style*. A further 25 per cent thought the answer was *both equally*.

Moreover, as we found in our research at the time, most people had not yet made up their mind about their new leader but were prepared in the meantime to give him the benefit of the doubt. Positive remarks nearly always concerned what people hoped he would be able to do or what he would turn out to be like, rather than what he was actually doing.

This was true throughout the summer – even by mid-September, although he had not done anything particularly inspirational, it was still too early to tell how Mr Brown would turn out. A different and rather less engaging style from Mr Blair's was already evident, though: while there seemed to be less spin going on, the new Prime Minister seemed rather nondescript and dowdy, and uncomfortable in the limelight.

This pattern of opinion in the first three months – a favourable attitude to Mr Brown based on hope and the benefit of the doubt, rather than tangible activity, and the absence of any reassessment of his underlying character – lent credence to a theory that had been bravely articulated by Anthony Wells on UK Polling Report nine months previously[44]. First, he predicted that the hypothetical increase in the Conservative lead that the polls suggested would appear at the handover would not, in fact materialise. Instead, Labour's share would rise significantly and they might even take the lead. In the longer term,

43   YouGov/*Daily Telegraph* poll, 19-21 September 2007, sample 2,085

44   'Gordon Brown – two predictions', www.ukpollingreport.com, 8 December 2006

though, Mr Brown would have the opposite effect on Labour's fortunes. The hypothetical polls – flawed for the sound methodological reasons outlined above – would in fact turn out to be right:

> [T]he present polls do say something about Brown's future success. If they showed people didn't like Brown because they doubted his competence or experience, or disagreed with his policies or principles, then it would be perfectly possible that Brown in office would change people's opinions, impress them with his competence or change their minds with new policies and ideas. Brown's negatives, though, are far more nebulous – they just don't *like* him. That will be very hard to change.

This theory was cold comfort to the Conservative Party during the extended Brown honeymoon of July, August and September 2007. The party had readied itself for a Brown Bounce, but became impatient with gravity. The Opposition was bound to suffer as the focus of attention switched to a new Prime Minister, but Conservative ratings had declined in absolute terms, not just relative. Some of this can be put down to the shifting spotlight – less airtime meant fewer opportunities for the party to show it understands ordinary people's problems, or is competent and capable. And less coverage of David Cameron, far and away the party's greatest asset, did not help the party's ratings or his own.

The Tories could not blame these circumstances alone. On 16 May David Willetts set out the Conservative policy on expanding the government's academy schools programme, a footnote of which was that a new Conservative government would not seek to open new grammar schools. There followed an internal but all too public row that was entirely self-inflicted and avoidable.

Little would go right for the Conservatives. At the end of July Mr Cameron went to Rwanda, where he took part in development projects, met President Kagame and made a major speech to the Rwandan parliament. The visit should have been a showcase for the Conservatives' approach to international development, the party's commitment to practical social action projects and its leader's growing profile on the international stage. But it coincided with record rainfall in West Oxfordshire and Mr Cameron was duly asked by a Rwandan television reporter: "What do you have to say about continuing with your visit to Rwanda when part of your constituency is completely devastated by floods?"

British journalists inevitably echoed the question. Yet if he had cancelled the trip (a very longstanding commitment), the political situation dictated that he would have faced equally unpalatable domestic headlines, doubtless featuring the words "beleaguered" and "panic".

Though Mr Cameron remained focused and unflappable, there was no doubt that the party was struggling to articulate a message during the Brown honeymoon. Most people remained well disposed to Mr Cameron personally but questions of substance and direction continued to emerge, as did the fear that he was the front man for a largely unchanged Conservative Party.

Politics being what it is, some Conservatives felt the answer was an all-out attack on Gordon Brown. Indeed a series of advertisements was developed, blaming the new Prime Minister for the problems Britain was facing after ten years of a government in which he had held the purse strings: Mr Brown was trying to position himself as the agent of change, and he was not to be allowed to get away with it (because if the government is the change, where does that leave the Opposition?). How could he be the change, when he sat in Cabinet where decisions were made, and when he signed the cheques for everything his predecessor did?

This approach was not a success. For one thing, people did not think it fair to blame Mr Brown for failures that had been outside his direct area of responsibility. More powerfully still, there was still a desire, even a determination, to let Mr Brown show what he could do even if this involved something of a suspension of disbelief.

Most importantly of all, the message failed not just because of what it said about Mr Brown but because of what it said about the Conservatives. People were eager to hear what the Conservatives had to say about their own plans, not about Labour. A message attacking Gordon Brown was bound not just to fail on its own terms, since people do not generally look to the Opposition for advice on what to think about the government; it would fail because if the best the Conservatives could do was complain about Gordon Brown then they clearly had nothing to say for themselves. (Not surprisingly, then, an alternative series of ads featuring David Cameron with positive statements about his principles and plans – on raising school standards, supporting families and sorting out the pension crisis – tested much more positively. While people debated the merits of the different proposals, they were at least left with the idea that there were proposals to debate.)

If talk of how the Conservatives should position Mr Brown was so much hot air, the task of positioning the Conservatives became more urgent. As the summer wore on, so did Labour's lead, and by September Labour had consolidated their position. This was no doubt helped by the Northern Rock crisis, in which the Bank of England provided emergency financial support after the credit crunch cut off the bank's funding in the financial markets, and the Chancellor, Alistair Darling, announced that the government would guarantee all existing Northern Rock deposits.

The changing economic backdrop, which placed Gordon Brown firmly into his most comfortable and familiar territory and heightened the risk of change in the public mind, combined with Labour's formidable poll ratings to excite speculation that the Prime Minister was preparing to call a general election. An early election had long been mooted as a possibility, and the suspicion that some Labour figures were recommending such a course was confirmed with the publication of a memo from the pollster and strategist Philip Gould in the *Daily Mirror*. Writing before the handover, Lord Gould advised Gordon Brown that the next election would be difficult, voters wanted change, and consolidation was therefore too dangerous an option:

> We have to have a strategy of audacious advance. The best way of achieving this is to hold an early election after a short period of intense and compelling activity. A kind of "shock and awe strategy" blasting through the opposition and blasting us to the mid-40 per-cents. It is inconceivable to me that you will not enjoy a significant honeymoon when you become leader. You need to build on this and translate it into a new mandate. I am sure this strategy will work.[45]

By the late summer, election fever dominated political discussion and by the end of September Cabinet ministers were openly weighing up the odds of going early and capitalising on current circumstances, or holding on and hoping the outlook remained favourable: Schools Secretary Ed Balls told the *Today* programme that "it's an interesting question as to where the gamble really lies". Mr Brown himself did nothing to dampen the excitement, telling one audience: "I think the first person I would have to talk to is the Queen."[46]

45   *Daily Mirror*, 2 August 2009
46   *Daily Telegraph*, 27 September 2007

The Conservatives had no choice but to say they welcomed the prospect of an election, but there was no public clamour to go to the polls. Many of the floating voters in our groups did not want to be asked to decide until they had had time to judge. In poll questions – at least those that did not include a one-sided preamble reminding participants that the Prime Minister had no democratic mandate – demand for an election was also muted. A YouGov poll for Channel 4 News found only 29 per cent thinking it was in the best interests of Britain to have the election *this autumn*, with 39 per cent preferring to hold on until 2008, and a further 18 per cent content to wait for 2009 or 2010.[47]

On Monday 1st October, at the Conservative Party conference, George Osborne announced that the next Tory government would raise the threshold for Inheritance Tax to £1 million. The announcement electrified the conference, and polls published in the following days found clear majorities in favour of the policy. Support was not confined to those groups most likely to benefit directly: according to YouGov[48] 60 per cent of people in social groups C2DE considered raising the threshold to £1 million to be a good policy, compared to 71 per cent of ABC1s. BPIX[49] found 71 per cent in favour of the policy, even though only one in five expected to inherit enough to pay the tax at the existing threshold of £300,000, and only one in three expected to leave enough for their children to be liable. David Cameron closed the conference with an unscripted 67-minute oration, concluding with a challenge to Gordon Brown to "go ahead and call that election".

Gordon Brown, meanwhile, began to make a series of unforced errors for the first time in his premiership. First, he went to Basra to announce that a thousand British troops would return from Iraq by Christmas. It quickly emerged that half of these had been accounted for in a previous announcement in September, and 270 of the troops in question were already home. Later in the week he visited Basildon to cut the ribbon at a medical centre which had already been treating patients for three months. Whether or not these items on the Prime Minister's schedule were deliberately designed to distract attention from the Tories, they did nothing to enhance the reputation for straightforwardness that had been one of Mr Brown's most important assets.

47   YouGov/Channel 4 poll, 24-25 September 2007, sample 1,341

48   YouGov/*Sunday Times* poll, 5-6 October 2007, sample 1,757

49   BPIX/*Mail on Sunday* poll, 3-5 October 2007, sample 2,059

As the Conservative conference progressed, the question of a general election remained at the front of all political minds. We expected the Prime Minister to visit Her Majesty in the second week of October, with polling day on November the first.

In a fireside chat on the afternoon of Saturday 6 October, the Prime Minister announced his decision to Andrew Marr and the nation:

> I'll not be calling an election and let me explain why. I have a vision for change in Britain. I want to show people how in government we are implementing it. Over the summer months we have had to deal with crises. We have had to deal with foot and mouth, terrorism, floods, the financial crisis. And yes we could have had an election on competence and I hope people would have understood that we have acted competently. But what I want to do is show people the vision that we have for the future of this country: in housing, health, education. And I want the chance in the next phase of my premiership to develop and show people the policies that will make a huge difference and show the change in the country itself.[50]

On the day of the announcement, news emerged of an ICM poll for that weekend's *News Of The World* putting Labour six points behind in the 83 most marginal constituencies (44 per cent to 38 per cent), a result that could have cost Labour 49 seats.

Two other polls published on the Sunday put the Conservatives ahead for the first time since Mr Brown became Prime Minister: BPIX in the *Mail On Sunday*,[51] by 39 per cent to 38 per cent, and YouGov in the *Sunday Times*,[52] by 41 per cent to 38 per cent. YouGov conducted the fieldwork for this poll on 5 and 6 October; on the previous two days they had carried out a poll for Channel 4 News which found a Labour lead of 4 points;[53] the previous weekend[54] YouGov had found a Labour lead of 11 points (43 per cent to 32 per cent).

---

50   Gordon Brown, BBC interview with Andrew Marr, 6 October 2007
51   BPIX/*Mail on Sunday poll*, 3-5 October 2007, sample 2,059
52   YouGov/*Sunday Times* poll, 5-6 October 2007, sample 1,757
53   YouGov/*Channel 4 News* poll, 3-4 October 2007, sample 1,741
54   YouGov/*Daily Telegraph* poll, 26-28 September 2007, sample 2,165

Evidently the Conservative conference halted Labour's advance. The Inheritance Tax proposal was popular, and David Cameron's speech had prompted people to start saying "he's got something about him": not just because of the extraordinary boldness of its delivery but because talking for over an hour without the help of a spin-doctor's script might just mean he meant what he was saying. But it was Gordon Brown's decision to cancel the general election that drove momentum in the other direction. "Chicken Saturday" compelled people to question the Prime Minister's reputation as a strong and decisive leader. To make matters even worse, Mr Brown doggedly insisted in the following days that the polls had played no part in his decision to cancel the election that he had evidently been planning for months.

Voters greeted this claim with contempt. More than half (52 per cent) of respondents in a YouGov poll[55] agreed that by making this assertion *Gordon Brown treated the British people like fools*, and more agreed (46 per cent) than disagreed (39 per cent) that *Mr Brown has emerged as a man who dithers and cannot make up his mind*. ICM[56] found 29 per cent saying their opinion of him had gone down over the previous month.

We found that people were beginning to reassess Mr Brown's character and performance. Previously, swing voters had hoped he would deliver on the basis of his strong image and performance as Chancellor, and meanwhile gave him the benefit of the doubt; now they wondered whether he was up to the job.

The impact of a political drama of the kind witnessed in October 2007 goes beyond headlines. In terms of brand, the underlying way in which people think about the parties and their leaders, the week's events could not have been more important. Gordon Brown's challenge on taking office had been to restore the standing of a government that had lost public trust. If his chief assets in the public mind were strength, competence and straightforwardness, the election decision and the reasons he gave for it suggested weakness, dithering and blatant falsehood. David Cameron, meanwhile, had reminded voters what they had liked about him in the first place with echoes of the 2005 party conference speech that had first brought him to the nation's attention as a different kind of Conservative leader. He had assuaged some doubts about his strength as a leader by showing he was up for a fight, and the fact that the poll reversal was due in part to a firm policy proposal went some way to addressing his party's supposed lack of substance.

55   YouGov/*Daily Telegraph* poll, 22-24 October 2007, sample 2,106
56   ICM/*Guardian* poll, 26-28 October 2007, sample 1,011

Mr Brown must kick himself to this day that he did not pre-empt the conference season by calling an election to capitalise on the comfortable Labour leads of the summer, while his ratings were high, Tory morale was low, and the public were more than willing to give him the benefit of the doubt. Even if he had gone to the Palace the week after the Conservative conference in October, I think he would still have won. The announcement would have come with the Conservatives no more than 3 points ahead in any national poll (indeed a Populus poll for *The Times* conducted over the weekend of 4-5 October found a 2-point Labour lead). There is no reason to think the 6-point lead found by ICM in marginal seats was wrong, but this could well have been overhauled during the course of a campaign.

Before he called off the election there remained a willingness to give Mr Brown a chance over the longer term, despite the lack of tangible progress since June. By going to the country, he would have rewarded the electorate's patience with a bold decision to seek his own mandate despite tightening polls, enhancing his underlying reputation for strength, rather than inviting a hail of mockery and derision for his apparent weakness and dithering. Conservative Campaign Headquarters would have spent October implementing a hastily assembled and inevitably imperfect general election campaign, rather than gleefully designing labels for Bottler Brown Ale with matching beer mats.

The "Bottler Brown" beermat
(I wish they wouldn't do this sort of thing. *MAA*)

And despite David Cameron's well-received speech and the success of the Inheritance Tax policy, the feeling up until that time was that the case had not yet been convincingly made for a Conservative government. There was no national impatience to change a Prime Minister who had been in office for just 14 weeks. I doubt that Labour's margin of victory would have been anything like the ten or eleven points some polls suggested at the end of September – David Cameron's performance and his profile on the campaign trail, compared to his relative obscurity while the country was absorbed with the newly elevated Mr Brown, would have seen to that. But it is hard to see how the Conservatives could have won a majority given the doubts about the party that had only begun to dissipate days before an election would have been called.

It is said that oppositions don't win elections, governments lose them. In fact, both conditions have to be met. From Saturday 6 October 2007 – albeit with the benefit of hindsight – one of those conditions was in place.

Boom and bust

The lead on the economy that saw Labour through two parliaments and halfway into a third was not built in opposition. Throughout the 1997 election campaign, ICM found the party neck and neck with the Conservatives, and a month before the election, MORI[57] found the Conservatives seven points ahead on the economy even though trailing by 15 points in voting intention. Only in the following months, safely in government and able to prove rather than claim their credentials, did they establish a reputation for economic competence.

As late as the summer of 2007, voters took the strong economy for granted. People largely accepted Gordon Brown's claim to have fostered stability, though they grumbled about stealth taxes and wasted government spending. Though some worried that the country's prosperity was precarious, there was no widespread fear that the economy was seriously vulnerable, let alone on the brink of recession. Certainly they felt no need to change the management. In that month's YouGov poll[58] for the *Daily Telegraph*, a clear

57   MORI poll, 8 April 1997
58   YouGov poll for the *Daily Telegraph*, 24-26 August 2007, sample 2,266

majority expected the financial situation of their household to stay the same or improve over the following year, with only 38 per cent expecting it to get worse. Forty per cent named Labour as the party most likely to run the economy well, twelve points ahead of the Conservatives.

Though this was at the height of Mr Brown's honeymoon, and most indicators favoured Labour, the Conservatives retained an advantage on law and order, immigration, "yobbish behaviour and street violence", and tied on tax and council tax – suggesting that Labour's lead on the economy in general was real enough. The government was also comfortably ahead when it came to inflation and interest rates.

The Northern Rock affair, the harbinger of the full economic crisis that was still a year away, began to unfold on 13 September when it emerged that the Bank of England had stepped in. Customers withdrew more than £2 billion in the first run on a British bank for more than a century. The run continued until the Chancellor, Alistair Darling, announced on 17 September that the government would guarantee all existing Northern Rock deposits.

The Conservatives backed the decision to support Northern Rock but argued that the government's management of the economy in recent years had left Britain particularly vulnerable to the effects of the credit crunch. George Osborne said the more fundamental question was "why Gordon Brown allowed the creation over 10 years of an economy built on debt, with consumer borrowing trebled and the largest budget deficit in Europe, in a way that threatens the broader stability of the economy".[59] The government argued that the credit crunch was the result of problems in the US sub-prime mortgage market, and that with low inflation, low interest rates, sixty consecutive quarters of economic growth and a strong regulatory framework, Britain was well placed to deal with instability in the financial markets.[60]

Voters were inclined to give the government the benefit of the doubt. The Northern Rock crisis and problems in the financial markets dominated the news and the prevailing view among the public was that things were about to get very much worse. But few at this stage were inclined to blame Mr Brown or his Chancellor; the culprits were the banks, particularly American ones. Though some felt the government should have acted earlier, it seemed to have done what was necessary.

---

59   *Express*, 15 September 2007
60   Alistair Darling statement (HM Treasury 95/07), 17 September 2007

The first poll to ask about Northern Rock[61] found 51 per cent saying the government had handled the issue *well* or *very well*, with only 29 per cent thinking it had done so *poorly*. Fifty-nine per cent named Gordon Brown as the party leader they most trusted to run the economy, with only 19 per cent choosing David Cameron. Similarly, Ipsos MORI[62] found 42 per cent declaring themselves *very* or *fairly satisfied*, with a further 21 per cent *neither satisfied nor dissatisfied*. Only a quarter were dissatisfied. When asked *Which team of leaders do you have more confidence in to handle a similar problem in the future?*, more than half (54 per cent) said Gordon Brown and Alistair Darling; only 22 per cent chose David Cameron and George Osborne.

If the effect of this first chapter of the financial crisis was to strengthen Labour's position, events after the cancelled election of October 2007 began to erode it. On 20 November Alistair Darling announced to the House of Commons that HMRC had contrived to lose the bank details of 25 million people – all recipients of Child Benefit, meaning every family in the country with children up to the age of 16. A series of similar embarrassing announcements ensued, including a confession by Ruth Kelly, then Transport Secretary, that the DVLA had lost the details of three million learner drivers. For the first time the public began to entertain doubts about the government's basic competence. More than half of voters thought the Chancellor was to some extent to blame for the HMRC fiasco, and 49 per cent thought the same of the Prime Minister.[63] While people were more likely to think Gordon Brown and Alistair Darling were competent at running the economy than David Cameron and George Osborne would be (though only by 51 per cent to 46 per cent), 42 per cent thought the government team incompetent – five points above the level who thought the same of the Tories. Comparisons were even drawn with the previous administration: BPIX[64] found more than half of voters thinking Mr Darling was doing worse than Norman Lamont, or no better; Gordon Brown was seen as less competent than John Major.

By the end of November, YouGov[65] found the Conservatives edging ahead of Labour on being more likely to run the economy well – albeit by only one point, and with more

61   ICM/*Sunday Mirror* poll, 19-21 September 2009, sample 1,029.

62   Ipsos MORI/*Sun* poll, 20-22 September 2007, sample 1,009.

63   YouGov poll for Channel 4, 21-22 November 2007, sample 1,600.

64   BPIX poll for the *Mail on Sunday*, 22-24 November 2007, sample 1,333.

65   YouGov poll for the *Daily Telegraph*, 26-28 November 2007, sample 1,966.

people saying *neither* or *don't know* than naming the Conservatives. Fifty-three per cent thought the unfortunate Mr Darling was doing a bad job as Chancellor, six points behind the proportion who were dissatisfied with Mr Brown as Prime Minister. More than half thought the government had so far done a *poor* or *awful* job on Northern Rock, to which it had by now lent some £25 billion, with only 37 per cent thinking its handling had been *fair* or better. Nearly two thirds said they were very or somewhat worried about the prospect of a recession in the next few months, and 60 per cent had not much confidence or none at all in the government's ability to deal with a downturn if it came. Just over a third agreed with the statement: *Although it has had a fair amount of bad luck recently, the present government is basically competent and efficient.* More than half chose the alternative: *The present government is neither competent nor efficient: to put it bluntly, it couldn't run a whelk stall.*

On 17 February 2008, after a series of jumps in the scale of taxpayer support for Northern Rock, the Chancellor announced that the bank would be nationalised. The Liberal Democrats had long advocated such a move, but the Conservatives opposed it: George Osborne said he would "not help Gordon Brown take this country back to the 1970s". He argued that the decision had been the culmination of a long period of dithering – a charge that had regularly been made against the Prime Minister since the cancelled election four months previously.

Sixty per cent of voters thought the Northern Rock management bore the most responsibility for the bank's difficulties, and a further 14 per cent blamed international financial conditions. One in ten blamed bank regulators and only 5 per cent thought the government was most responsible.[66] Though most people agreed that ministers had taken far too much time to decide what to do about the situation, and were evenly divided over whether nationalisation was the right course, 63 per cent thought the Conservatives would have handled the crisis either no better or worse. Less than a third thought the reason for the Conservatives' opposition to the government's solution was that *they genuinely think nationalisation is the wrong policy and would probably do something different if they were in office*; more than half assumed the party was *"playing politics" and would probably do much the same as the government are doing now if they were in office.*

This was to become a familiar pattern of opinion as the financial crisis took hold: public uncertainty, even anxiety, about the government's actions, but bafflement as to what other

66   YouGov poll for *The Economist*, 18-20 February 2010, sample 2,118

options were available and doubt that the opposition had any credible alternative plan. Another element of public perception was established early on: the judgment that, however well they may or may not be handling it, the crisis could not reasonably be said to be all the government's fault. Asked at the end of March 2008[67] which factors they thought were most to blame for the worsening economic situation, 52 per cent named *the worldwide "credit crunch"*, with 22 per cent blaming the policies Gordon Brown pursued as Chancellor and only eight per cent blaming his current policies as Prime Minister. People were more inclined to see government policies as secondary factors, but when asked to name the top two causes the credit crunch was still named more often than Mr Brown's actions, past or present. At the same time, 59 per cent did not think the government was handling the situation properly.

The credit crunch had entered the public lexicon and added to a gathering mood of pessimism. The economic concern that was closest to home for most people was the rising cost of living, particularly when it came to petrol and food prices and utility bills. With the exception of petrol prices (which were universally agreed to be down to extortionate tax rates), most people still did not blame the government for the causes of the downturn, but they still expected ministers to do something about it. Regardless of Labour's record of managing the economy over the previous decade (which several were now beginning for the first time to think was open to question), it was the government's actions now in the face of the current crisis that counted. Many, though, felt that it was failing on this score. The government had not done enough to foresee and guard against the impact of the credit crunch, and did not seem to understand how tough people were finding things, and by insisting that the economy was stable and growing was increasingly showing itself to be out of touch. The scrapping of the 10p starting rate of income tax in the March Budget had added to this impression (and the measures the Chancellor introduced to compensate low earners in response to the subsequent uproar added charges of weakness and confusion to those of insensitivity and poor judgment). For many, Gordon Brown's advice in July that people would find their living costs easier to control if they stopped wasting so much food perfectly illustrated ministers' increasing detachment from ordinary people's reality.

Most polls over the summer of 2008 found Conservative leads in the upper teens or above, and in one celebrated but wholly misleading case as high as 28 points.[68] The events

67   YouGov poll for the *Daily Telegraph*, 26-27 March 2008, sample 1,926
68   Ipsos MORI, 12-14 September 2008, sample 1,017 (Con 52%, Lab 24%, Lib Dem 12%)

of that autumn, though, lent a new perspective. At the end of August Alistair Darling warned that the economic conditions facing Britain were "arguably the worst they've been in 60 years", and that the effects would be "more profound and long-lasting than people thought".[69] Some time later Mr Darling would say that 10 Downing Street responded by unleashing the "forces of hell" against him, but events in the banking sector quickly began to suggest that he was right. On 15 September, Lehman Brothers filed for bankruptcy, on 17 September competition law was bypassed to allow Lloyds TSB to take over the collapsing HBOS, on 29 September the government announced the nationalisation of Bradford & Bingley after investors and lenders lost confidence in its ability to continue as an independent institution, on 8 October Gordon Brown announced a £400 billion rescue package for British banks, and on 13 October the government injected £37 billion of capital into RBS, Lloyds TSB and HBOS.

The crisis left the public gloomy and uncertain. People expected the situation to worsen before it improved, and in a YouGov poll[70] in early October, more than half of voters expected a recession. Ninety per cent described the state of the economy as "quite bad" or "very bad" (0 per cent of the 1,941 respondents described it as "very good"). However, people were much more pessimistic about the prospects for the British economy generally than for their own households. In a Populus poll for *The Times* in early November[71], people were pessimistic about the economy for the country as a whole by 66 to 31 per cent; asked how the economy would fare for them and their family, more were optimistic (51 per cent) than pessimistic (44 per cent).

As for the bank bailout, polls suggested that the package had a reasonable degree of public support. In the YouGov poll, 59 per cent said the multi-billion pound bank rescue plan was *probably necessary if Britain's financial system was not to collapse*, with only 32 per cent opposing on the grounds that *taxpayers should not bail out the banks*. As we found in our own research, the truth was that people were in fact very uneasy about the bailouts – which involved unimaginable amounts of money and entailed consequences that were impossible to predict – but had no idea what the alternative was, or whether there was one. Unlike other more straightforward political controversies on which they could confidently offer a

69   Alistair Darling interview with the *Guardian*, 30 August 2008

70   YouGov poll for the *Sunday Times*, 9-10 October 2008, sample 1,941

71   Populus poll for *The Times*, 7-9 October 2008, sample 1,503

view – such as putting more police on the beat to cut crime – people found themselves in the uncomfortable position of just having to hope the government knew what it was doing.

The same was true when it came to the government's proposed stimulus package, whose details were announced in the Chancellor's Pre-Budget Report the following month. The Conservatives argued that the plan was unaffordable. Voters agreed that borrowing more to increase public spending to keep the economy going sounded like an expensive gamble. But again, what was the alternative?

Though some criticised the government for failing to anticipate the crisis or take steps to prevent it, and the evident lack of effective regulation, most people still did not blame Gordon Brown. Indeed two polls[72] at the beginning of October found that people were at least as inclined to blame the government of the United States as they were to blame their own ministers. Populus also found people attaching more responsibility to *people who took out loans and mortgages they couldn't really afford* than to the British government. American banks and mortgage lenders were held to be the guiltiest party by far.

Conservative attempts to persuade voters that they should blame Labour for the wider economic situation made little headway. Though people were more ready to accept than dismiss the Conservative charge that the Labour government "didn't fix the roof when the sun was shining", most thought things would have been done no differently had the Conservatives been in office during this time, and some thought they would have done even worse on this score. There was no sense that the financial crisis would have been avoided, or that the response would have been any different, had the Tories been in charge.

The size of the crisis, the lack of a clear domestic culprit, and people's confusion (to which they readily admitted) about the policies the government was putting in place, meant that they had to rely on instinct when deciding whom to trust to get us out of the mess. Incumbency was undoubtedly an advantage for Labour at this point. Gordon Brown was back on his home territory of the economy, and though he was later ridiculed for a slip of the tongue at Prime Minister's Questions in which he seemed to claim to have "saved the world", his apparently leading role at the G7 Summit in October and in other discussions with international leaders at least made it look as though he was doing something, even if it was impossible for people to say whether his frenetic activity would make any difference.

---

72   YouGov poll for the *Daily Telegraph*, 1-3 October 2008, sample 2,048; Populus poll for *The Times*, 3-5 October 2008, sample 1,503

Consequently, though there was no real improvement in perceptions of Mr Brown's overall performance as Prime Minister, the view that his experience as Chancellor put him in a position to steer Britain through the crisis gained ground. In mid-October both YouGov and ICM found 61 per cent thinking Mr Brown had been handling the crisis "quite well" or "very well" over the preceding few weeks. [73] ICM also found that people trusted Gordon Brown and Alistair Darling to handle the crisis rather than David Cameron and George Osborne by 43 to 35 per cent.[74]

The Conservatives made a number of positive proposals during this time, including a temporary cut in employers' National Insurance contributions, allowing firms to defer VAT payments for six months, a new Office of Budget Responsibility to help safeguard the public finances, and later a national loan guarantee scheme to help firms secure finance. The fact that voters remained largely unaware of any such ideas, let alone a more general Conservative economic theme, was partly due to the perennial difficulty of getting a message heard. This task was made much more difficult by the fact that the balance of the Conservative message on the economy, as heard by voters, was negative, suggesting that the party was more interested in criticising the government than putting forward an alternative. The following, interspersed with rather more occasional positive stories, are some headlines from Shadow Cabinet press releases on the economy in October and November 2008, and they give a flavour of the party's economic message as the voters heard it: "We are all paying the price of Labour's failure", "Unemployment the result of Brown's Age of Irresponsibility", "Brown's foolish claim on the end of boom and bust", "Brown has failed to end boom and bust", "Labour's failure to prepare the economy will hit families", "Record collapse of the pound under Labour", "Brown is a man with an overdraft, not a plan", "Repossessions the tragic price of Labour's failure", "Brown won't admit his fiscal rules have collapsed", "Labour have maxed out Britain's credit card", "The truth about Labour's tax con is finally coming out", "Bankruptcies are the price of Brown's irresponsibility", "Labour failing to revive mortgage lending", "Brown's small business bombshell", "Families pay price for Labour's tax timebomb", "Gordon Brown has been found out", "Labour are playing havoc with the public purse".

---

73   YouGov poll for the *Mirror*, 15-17 October 2008, sample 2,029; ICM poll for the *Guardian*, 17-19 October 2008

74   ICM poll for the *News of the World*, 15-17 October 2008, sample 1,041

The absence of any clear perceived difference between the parties in their approach to the economy lent some credence to Gordon Brown's assertion in his Labour Conference speech that this was "no time for a novice". Most people felt strongly that it was time for a change, but also that it was far from clear what kind of change, if any, a Conservative government would bring. While "change" would beat "experience" – and most people accepted the argument David Cameron made in his own conference speech that if experience were the only important criterion Mr Brown would now have to be Prime Minister forever – this argument was somewhat less compelling if the alternative on offer was similar policies but less experienced people. Though willing to appoint a "novice" in order to get the change they felt the country needed, they were rather less willing to do so if they thought little change would result. Unfortunately for the Conservatives, this was the prevailing view. Accordingly, the Conservative poll lead fell from the high teens of the summer to end the year at around 5 points.

January 2009 brought the announcement of a second bank bailout and the news that Britain was officially in recession. This time the bad economic news did not prompt voters to prefer experience and the devil they knew: the Conservative lead climbed quickly back into double figures and stayed there for most of the year. ICM found that most people were uncomfortable with the government nationalising or buying large stakes in major banks, and that people were more likely to think its measures for combating the recession would make no difference (45 per cent) or even make things worse (19 per cent) than that they would improve the situation (31 per cent).[75] However, they still refused to blame the government. YouGov found more than half saying banks in Britain or America bore the largest responsibility for the problems facing the British economy, compared to only a fifth who thought Gordon Brown and his government to be the most culpable. Nearly two thirds agreed with the statement *The current crisis is global: whatever Britain did our economy would not have been able to avoid a downturn.*[76] The fact that voters put us ahead in the polls while still not blaming the government for the recession should have served as yet more evidence that our attacks on Labour's economic management were redundant.

Though the Prime Minister liked to contrast the "real help now" offered by the Labour government with the "do nothing Conservatives", the Tories regained the lead in most polls

75   ICM poll for the *Guardian*, 23-25 January 2009, sample 1,003

76   YouGov poll for the *Daily Telegraph*, 27-29 January 2009, sample 2,338

on overall economic management. But longstanding brand perceptions meant there were nuances within this picture. In an ICM[77] poll in March, people thought the economy was more likely to deteriorate, and taxes were more likely to go up, under Labour, while Britain would come out of recession more quickly under the Conservatives. At the same time, though, big cuts in public services were more likely under the Tories, and income would be spread more evenly under Labour.

In April the Chancellor unveiled a record budget deficit of £175 billion. The debate over debt and how to deal with it, which was to dominate discussion of the economy until the election and beyond, proved a minefield as far as public opinion was concerned. First, there was the question of what the debt actually was. When politicians talked about the debt crisis, for example, they were usually talking about what was owed by the government. The audience did not always realise this. Terms like "the public finances" are opaque to most people, and they did not tend to think of Britain's debt problem just in terms of the public sector: it encompassed excessive credit card borrowing, reckless mortgages and irresponsible bank lending. This meant that attempts to label the issue as "Labour's debt crisis" or "Gordon Brown's debts" sounded particularly unreasonable – why is it Labour's fault if someone borrows more than they can afford or a bank makes bad loans?

Few people understood what government debt meant in practice. What does it mean if the government, or Britain, owes money? Who lends it to us? What will happen if we don't pay it back? Why don't we just tell them to get stuffed? Partly for this reason, although huge government debt sounded serious and vaguely worrying, there was no intuitive grasp of the potential effect on the real economy, let alone on people's family finances. The fact that the government was spending more on debt interest than on schools was a good illustration that helped to show the practical cost of the deficit, but the idea that too much government borrowing would ultimately mean higher mortgage rates was a step beyond most people's understanding. And the size of the sums involved – a trillion pounds by 2014 – were so huge as to be meaningless.

The debt crisis, despite being the single most important economic question of the time, therefore had an air of unreality to many voters. But if they did not feel the immediacy of the problem, the potential solutions felt much closer to home. Most people instinctively favoured the Conservative argument that the debt crisis was so serious that action had to be taken to reduce borrowing immediately (rather than the Labour view that early action would jeopardise the recovery). Most polls also showed a preference for the emphasis to be on spending cuts rather than tax rises. While tackling the deficit was urgent in theory and spending cuts were fine in principle, spending cuts in practice were a rather different matter.

The incomprehensibility of the numbers involved made it impossible for people to calibrate potential solutions. Consequently they were prone to overestimate the potential savings to be made from cutting things they disapproved of. Just as, a decade earlier, people thought the NHS could be funded for a year on the money that would be saved by scrapping the Millennium Dome, surely the current problem could be solved by clamping down on MPs' expenses, dealing with scroungers, banning bonuses in newly state-owned banks and sorting out the ubiquitous public sector waste. Cuts to services people actually used, or benefits they actually received, were inevitably a less welcome prospect – particularly given the rather distant and, as far as they were concerned, intangible nature of the budget deficit.

A study by Policy Exchange[78] captured this point very effectively. Offered four ways in which the government could balance the books – raising taxes, cutting spending, or different combinations of the two – only a quarter chose options involving tax rises and two thirds chose spending cuts. Asked later how they would adjust the budget for each department, participants demanded *more* spending on pensions, health, schools, police, roads, rail and defence.

Some Conservative MPs and commentators argued forcefully for the party to propose bold cuts in public spending. In doing so they often claimed that the public shared their enthusiasm. Fraser Nelson, for example, reported in the *Spectator* that a study[79] had found 72 per cent agreeing that the government *spends much too much* or *a little too much money on programmes and services*. This was a very partial reading of what the survey actually found, which was 72 per cent agreeing with the statement *The government currently spends much/a little too much money on programmes and services – there is wastage everywhere/there are some pockets of wastage*. Leaving aside the very odd wording of the question (the response would perhaps have been different had it read "programmes like Child Benefit and services like the NHS"), all this shows is that people think the government wastes a lot of money – hardly

78   *Tax and Spending: Views of the British Public*, Neil O'Brien, Policy Exchange, 1 October 2009

79   'Are spending cuts back? A deliberative study', PoliticsHome in association with the *Spectator*, April 2009

the same thing as a demand for real reductions, and hardly showing, as the *Spectator* article claimed, that "the public is way ahead of Cameron in seeing the need for cuts".

The report also purported to show a strong shift in opinion towards lower public spending since the last election. Unfortunately it did this by comparing five very different questions over four years. In January 2005, for example, when YouGov asked *Do you believe taxes should be cut, or should any money available for tax cuts be used to increase public spending on public services such as health and education?*, 57 per cent chose higher spending. Three years later, given the preamble *Taking everything into account do you think the overall amount of money that the government raises in taxation is… ,* 67 per cent chose the answer *Too high; the government should tax less and spend less.* Spend less on what – health and education? People are much more likely to agree that government spending needs to be cut if you do not remind them in the question what the spending pays for. These two questions would have produced vastly different answers if they had been asked on the same day, yet the report claimed that they helped to prove that "the direction of travel away from higher public spending is clear", even "a new landscape of public opinion on tax and spend".

Even if it had been true that the public favoured lower spending, appearing to be over-eager to cut would have been a dangerous approach for the Conservatives to follow. The report found the two most resonant attacks on the Conservative Party were *The Tories are the party of millionaires, offering tax cuts for the wealthy while others suffer*, and – guess what – *The Tories are the party of spending cuts and slashing public services.* Arguing that cuts were necessary was one thing, and it was true that the public reluctantly accepted this in principle, as a necessary evil, and were ready to hear an honest assessment from politicians about how bad things were going to be. But cuts themselves were never popular, and for the Conservatives to campaign as though they were would have been very damaging.

If real cuts were necessary, who was best placed to make them? Again, brand perceptions played a much bigger role here than anything specifically set out by either party. Though the Conservatives retained their lead on managing the economy in most polls, the ruthless streak that made them more likely than the other parties to eliminate waste[80]

---

80   Being thought more likely than the other parties to cut waste does not amount to a very high degree of expectation: cutting waste often sounded to people like a generic political promise, like putting more bobbies on the beat.

also predisposed them to make bigger and more damaging cuts. ICM[81] found in June that while most people thought the Conservatives were *likely to reduce government borrowing*, more disagreed than agreed that they were *likely to protect public services*. The following month they found that while the Conservatives were much more likely than Labour to cut spending *about the right amount*, they were also more likely to cut *too much*.[82]

At the Conservative Party Conference in October George Osborne began to set out some of the areas in which savings would be made: he would freeze public sector pay, end means tested tax credits for those earning more than £50,000, and bring forward the date at which the retirement age was set to rise. In addition, to show that we were "all in this together", the Conservatives would cut ministers' pay by 5 per cent, cut the number of MPs, limit top public sector pensions, cut the cost of Whitehall by a third, and keep, for the time being, the 50 per cent income tax rate on earnings over £150,000.

The Conservatives were given some credit for being open about the cuts that were on the way. Already they had been more specific on this point than Labour. Though it cuts little ice with voters, there is some truth in the idea that the Opposition cannot give detailed plans because it has not seen the books. For this reason, Mr Osborne was limited in the degree of detail – and therefore the degree of reassurance – that he was able to offer. The Tories had promised to protect the budgets for the NHS and (oddly, as far as many voters were concerned) international development. But since the savings needed would clearly have to go beyond what Mr Osborne had presented, where would the other cuts fall?

Since neither party was in a position to present a full Budget for the following year even if they had wanted to, voters' judgment would come down to trust and values. Shortly after the Conference, Populus[83] found a small advantage for the Conservatives when it came to making cuts *with the interests of ordinary people at heart*, and an even split of opinion on who would cut *in ways that protect frontline public services*. Labour had a clear lead on *minimising the number of public sector job losses* and *spreading the burden of cuts fairly so that the best off bear their share too*. ICM[84] found people more likely to think the Conservatives would cut *about the right amount* than Labour (by 38 to 28 per cent). But the Conservatives

---

81   ICM poll for the *Guardian*, 12-14 June 2009, sample 1,006

82   ICM poll for the *Guardian*, 10-11 July 2009

83   Populus poll for *The Times*, 9-11 October 2009, sample 1,504

84   ICM poll for the *Guardian*, 16-18 October 2009, sample 1,002

were also more likely to be expected to cut *too much* (by 34 to 28 per cent). And while southern voters were considerably more likely to think the Tories would cut the right amount than to cut too much, those in the north were evenly divided.

In the 2009 Budget the Chancellor confirmed his intention, announced the previous year, to increase National Insurance contributions by 1 per cent for employers and most employees. Conservative opposition to this plan became an important rallying call in the election campaign. The NI rise was described as a "tax on jobs" that would hold back the recovery – at a time when we needed to get the economy moving, the last thing we needed was to make it more expensive for firms to employ people. This was a much more persuasive argument than a simple promise of lower taxes that would save people a few hundred pounds a year (which experience, hardened into cynicism, tells them never to take at face value). The cost of the Conservative plan would be met by finding an extra £6 billion in efficiency savings. The inevitable difficulty in being specific about these savings made some people nervous, either because they would involve unpalatable cuts or because the savings would not materialise and taxes would rise elsewhere. Overall, though, the NI policy did more good than harm, lending weight to the Conservative message on creating growth and illustrating the link between debt, waste and higher taxes. Interestingly, one aspect of the message that was a brilliant success in operational terms – the collection of hundreds of business endorsements for the Conservative policy, including dozens from famous names – left the voters nonplussed. The endorsements helped to generate news, and added to the policy's credibility among commentators, all of which made the exercise worthwhile. But voters saw it simply as a series of business people supporting what was in their own private interests. There might well be good reasons to support the policy, but the fact that it would make certain businessmen richer was not one of them.

It has been widely noted that some of the Conservatives' best moments in the years before the 2010 election involved tax, or more specifically, tax cuts: the 2007 pledge to raise the Inheritance Tax threshold to £1 million, opposing the abolition of the 10p income tax band, and reversing the planned National Insurance rise. Each of these certainly helped the Conservatives, to different degrees. The argument that is often implied, though, is this: since proposing tax cuts obviously works, think how much better the Tories would have done if they had promised an overall tax cut. This is to misread the reasons why these three particular policies were so powerful. Each one had particular features that helped Conservative arguments to resonate with the public. With Inheritance Tax, it was the breathtaking unfairness, as most people saw it, of having to pay tax once when they earned their money and again when they tried to leave it to their family.[85] With the scrapping of the 10p tax rate, it was the fact that the change would only hit people on the very lowest incomes (since the basic rate of income tax was reduced from 22p to 20p). With the National Insurance rise, as argued above, it was the risk of adding to the cost of employing people at a time when it was essential to create jobs.

A pledge to cut taxes overall would have been a completely different proposition. David Cameron and George Osborne were derided for their refusal to make such a promise, and for insisting on the need to put "economic stability before tax cuts", but this was the right call. A guarantee of upfront tax cuts would have been greeted with the utmost suspicion, and would have undermined the message on our commitment to public services which was crucial to helping win over former Labour and Liberal Democrat voters. And had we adopted such a policy, the consequences for our credibility once the recession hit and debt became the inescapable fact of economic life hardly bear thinking about.

A MONTH BEFORE the election, Populus[86] found a six-point lead on managing the economy for David Cameron and George Osborne over Gordon Brown and Alistair Darling. The Conservative Party was thought more likely than Labour *to pay for its promises by cutting waste rather than by cutting services and jobs,* and *to represent the interests of people who work hard and play by the rules,* while Labour were more likely *to put up taxes for people like you.* However, Labour were more trusted than the Conservatives, particularly among swing voters, to *make cuts in ways that don't harm important public services and that minimise the negative impact on ordinary people.*

---

85   In fact voters were at least as exercised by the iniquity of double taxation in principle as by the fact that people of fairly modest means were finding themselves in the Inheritance Tax net because of their family home. Many felt strongly that IHT should be scrapped altogether. When it was explained that the Conservative policy would mean only millionaires would pay the tax, people would very often ask what the party had against millionaires.

The pollster Deborah Mattinson reports in her book *Talking to a Brick Wall* that she found similar concern about Inheritance Tax in her research for Labour in 2007: first-generation property owners and their children "were outraged that this opportunity might be diminished by what they saw as a punitive and unfair tax on their family's achievement" (p. 171).

86   Populus poll for *The Times*, 6 April 2010, sample 1,507

During the campaign, this concern about the impact of impending cuts loomed larger in voters' thinking – no doubt because they now seemed imminent. The debt crisis and its implications had two principal effects in the campaign. First, it suggested that whoever was elected, the need to cut the deficit would mean their room for manoeuvre would be extremely limited. Combined with a continuing complaint that they did not know what sort of alternative approach to the economy was on offer, this led people to conclude that meaningful change was unlikely, probably for many years. This was often accompanied, with some justification, by the grumble that the Conservatives still seemed determined to focus on how Gordon Brown got us into the mess, rather than how they were going to get us out of it. Here is another batch of economy-themed press releases, this time between 1 January 2010 and the election: "Gordon Brown's legacy will be the Great Recession", "Labour's attacks on middle Britain", "Labour's recession hits manufacturing", "Over five million victims of Labour's jobs crisis", "Labour's two nations", "Gordon Brown's record", "Labour's empty Budget", "Brown's record £120 a month in council tax", "Growing fears of jobless recovery under Labour", "The biggest risk to Britain is five more years of Gordon Brown", "We can't afford another five years of Labour's incompetence", "Labour will kill the recovery". (Plus, not on the economy: "David Cameron criticises Labour's negativity".)

Second, it made people consider what impact the parties' likely approaches would have on them personally. People became increasingly worried, especially in the North, that rather than being proportionate and fair the Conservatives would cut deeply and with relish; Labour might at least try to soften the blow. Public sector workers, even if they wanted change and were leaning towards the Conservatives, began to ask themselves who was most likely to protect their job. People who received tax credits, which were closely associated with Labour, worried that they might be at risk under a Conservative government. Labour's campaign exploited and fuelled these fears.

In terms of policy, the Conservatives went into the election with a strong case on the economy. David Cameron and George Osborne correctly insisted on the need to deal with the deficit immediately, and were right to seek a mandate to do so. The prospect of cuts was never going to enthuse voters, but a more "blue skies" message on the economy would have risked sounding delusional. Having resisted calls for reckless tax promises earlier in the parliament, the Conservative economic approach was sufficiently robust to win endorsements from the *Economist* and the *Financial Times*. But doubts lingered about the party's motivation and priorities, leading to fears among many swing voters that a

Tory government's cuts would hurt them personally. The party's determination to convict Gordon Brown of responsibility for the economic crisis meant that many of those fears went unallayed.

Expenses

The cynical but widely held view that politicians had their snouts in the trough had been brewing for some time before the *Telegraph* revelations of May 2009. Public suspicion found regular confirmation in cases such as that of Derek Conway, who was suspended from the Commons in January 2008 for paying his son from public funds for no apparent work, and Michael Martin, who was criticised for claiming expenses for running a second home while living free in the Speaker's House, and investigated over reports that his wife had spent £4,000 of public money on taxis for shopping trips. Jacqui Smith was revealed to have designated her sister's spare bedroom as her main home, allowing her to claim expenses on her family home in Redditch, and she later repaid and apologised for a claim that covered two adult films. Tony McNulty was reported to have claimed £60,000 over twelve years by designating his parents' house in his Harrow constituency as his second home, when in fact he lived in Hammersmith.

Voters did not believe for a moment that revelations like this were isolated incidents. Far from being a small minority who abused the system, the miscreants represented a culture of stretching the rules to the limit and beyond. Shortly after the Conway scandal ICM[87] found only one in twenty saying they trusted MPs *a lot* to *obey financial rules regarding their own salaries and expenses*. Forty-one per cent trusted them *a little* but more than half trusted them *not at all*. In a YouGov poll[88] the following month, two thirds said they *tend to agree* with the statement *Most Members of Parliament make a lot of money by using public office improperly*. Nearly three quarters said they believed that many, most or all MPs *claim a significant amount of expenses improperly*.

This lack of public trust was compounded by MPs' apparent determination to conceal the details of the system that kept them in the manner to which they had become all

---

87   ICM poll for the *Sunday Telegraph*, 30-31 January 2008
88   YouGov poll for the *Daily Telegraph*, 26-27 February 2008, sample 2,011

too readily accustomed. The House of Commons vigorously opposed publication of the Additional Costs Allowance Guide, better known as the John Lewis List, which detailed the maximum amounts that could be reimbursed for various items. Voters reacted with indignation when the list was eventually revealed in March 2008. The sums involved were secondary – indeed, the smaller and more petty the claim, such as 88p for the Home Secretary's bath plug, the angrier they often made people. More important was the fact that MPs were allowed to claim for such items as a food mixer (£200) or a sideboard (£750) or the installation of a new bathroom (£6,335): what on earth did these things have to do with the work of an MP? There were no party distinctions – the antagonism was directed at parliamentarians as a breed. MPs' lives appeared completely detached from those of the people they were supposed to represent. How could they understand something like the rising cost of living when they were able to help themselves to dining chairs (£90 each) or install a new kitchen (£10,000) and send the bill to the taxpayer? Not only did MPs enjoy a completely different way of life, they didn't even have to pay for it.

If the John Lewis list provoked a reaction somewhere between mild irritation and grumpy resentment, the scandal that engulfed politics from 8 May 2009 unleashed something closer to cold fury. Most voters were not particularly surprised by the daily stream of outrages, but they were still shocked, and the anger was palpable. Again it was not the amounts of money for individual claims that incensed people, it was the systematic nature of the thing: the fact that MPs seemed to be claiming quite routinely, as expenses, things that apparently had nothing to do with their jobs and which many ordinary people could not afford. People had no truck with such trifles as the difference between expenses incurred in the course of an MP's work, and allowances designed to help meet the inevitable cost of living and working in two places. Nor did they draw a distinction between claims that were "within the rules" and claims that were not, because MPs themselves wrote the rules – rules that did not apply at most places of work. The point was that money left people's pockets in taxes and materialised in the form of assorted luxuries in MPs' lavishly appointed homes – second homes! – and gardens.

Property was the single element of the system that aroused the most ire: the fact that MPs could buy a house or flat, claim the mortgage interest, commission various works that enhanced its value at public expense, and sell it on at a profit. The practice of "flipping", where the constituency and then the London property was designated as the second home and therefore eligible for subsidy, meant this could be done more than once. This was clearly unacceptable. But many questioned why MPs needed a subsidy for a second home at all. Why couldn't they stay in a cheap hotel? Or why don't they build a hall of residence? And why do they need to claim for travel between London and their constituency? Other people can't claim the cost of going to work!

The ferocity of the public reaction, and the absolute refusal to give MPs the benefit of any doubt, were symptoms of the fact that this was not a first offence to be treated with lenience. This was the voters finally losing their patience, and their temper, with a political class that had in their view become steadily more remote and arrogant over the course of many years.[89] Though people did not have a clear or consistent view on how the system should be reformed (other than that it should be bracingly austere) they were unanimous on one point: that it should be independently administered and policed. People simply did not trust MPs with the task.

The relentlessness of the story seemed to prove what people had long suspected – that MPs were all at it, and that they were all as bad as each other. Populus[90] found 69 per cent thinking that at least a majority of MPs abused the system of expenses and allowances, including 27 per cent who thought that *all or nearly all MPs do it* (though only a third thought their own MP did so). In a YouGov[91] poll, 60 per cent agreed that *Most MPs have been deliberately abusing the allowances system and ripping us all off*. Only just over a third thought *Most MPs are reasonably honest, but a significant minority have been abusing the allowances system*. Just 2 per cent thought *Almost all MPs are reasonably honest; few, if any, have been abusing the allowances system*.

Though people could cheerfully recall the most sensational stories (duck house, moat cleaning) as well as long lists of those that had particularly amused or scandalised them (scatter cushions, bath plugs), they could rarely remember which MP was responsible for each, or even which party. In the polls, all three main parties were punished, particularly when it came to voting intention for the European Parliament elections on 4 June (which

---

89   Right on cue, the Commons authorities responded with their usual tin ear. When details first began to emerge Mr Speaker Martin declared he was "deeply disappointed", not with MPs but with the fact that the information had become public, and demanded an investigation into whether data protection laws had been broken. Voters thought the leaker had performed a valuable public service.

90   Populus poll for *The Times*, 3-5 April 2009, sample 1,512

91   YouGov poll for the *Sun*, 13-14 May 2009, sample 1,814

voters regard as an opportunity to administer a kicking without affecting anything that matters very much). Yet at a deeper level, the scandal affected the main parties in subtly different ways.

Labour bore the brunt of voters' rage. ICM and Populus polls in May[92] both found at least half of voters saying all parties had been damaged equally, but those thinking one party had been particularly damaged named Labour by a wide margin. In the Populus poll, 62 per cent named Gordon Brown as the leader who had been most badly hit, while only a quarter thought all three had suffered equally. A separate ICM poll,[93] which did not suggest in the question that all parties might have been equally affected, found more than half of respondents saying Labour had come off worst. Partly, this was because Labour were in charge and the scandal happened on their watch: if the rules needed to be changed, Labour as the governing party were in a position to change them. Gordon Brown's reaction also seemed slow and unsatisfactory, and failed to grasp the magnitude of the situation. The Prime Minister's YouTube broadcast of 23 April was noted mostly for his eccentric delivery and his proposal to replace the existing regime with a daily attendance allowance, prompting the objection that MPs would be paid extra simply for turning up to work. But his analysis of the problem missed the public mood: "Every MP I know wants to live by the rules but for too long some of these rules have been insufficiently clear." People did not believe that well-meaning MPs had been bamboozled by the system; they thought MPs were taking the public for a ride, and if they had created ambiguous rules they had done so quite deliberately. Finally, there was particular disappointment among Labour voters. You might expect this sort of sleaze from the Tories, they thought, but we expected better from Labour: Labour MPs are supposed to be on our side, they are supposed to be like us.

Liberal Democrat MPs seemed not to be responsible for many lurid stories (though some Liberal Democrat voters were saddened to find their party involved at all). Though they suffered in the polls, the Lib Dems were considered the least likely offenders. YouGov[94] found only 37 per cent thinking it *very likely* that *a typical Liberal Democrat MP has claimed money wrongly*, compared to 49 per cent for a typical Conservative and 59 per

---

92   ICM poll for the *Guardian*, 15-17 May 2009, sample 1,002; Populus poll for *The Times*, 27-28 May 2009, sample 1,001

93   ICM poll for the *Sunday Telegraph*, 27-28 May 2009, sample 1,013

94   YouGov poll for the *Daily Telegraph*, 14-16 May 2009, sample 2,235

cent for a typical Labour MP. The Populus poll found the Liberal Democrats and Nick Clegg to be the least damaged by a wide margin. At the same time, the ICM-*Guardian* poll found people evenly divided over whether Nick Clegg had handled the issue well or badly, with nearly a quarter saying *don't know*, and in the YouGov-*Sun* poll people had more confidence that David Cameron would act effectively to tackle the issue than the Lib Dem leader. If the Liberal Democrats were invisible on this particular story, no doubt they were content with that.

The effect of the expenses scandal on the Conservative Party was the most nuanced. All three leaders were criticised for failing to act until the scandal became public, but David Cameron was recognised as having given the earliest and most decisive response, pre-empting the independent Commons inquiry by imposing new rules on Conservative MPs, and ordering Shadow Cabinet members to repay controversial claims. He established a Scrutiny Panel to review excessive claims and decide what should be repaid: Conservative MPs would "pay back the money agreed or they will no longer be Conservative MPs".[95] This was rewarded in the polls – more than half of respondents in the YouGov-*Telegraph* poll thought David Cameron had *shown the most decisive leadership over MPs' expenses*. In the YouGov-*Sun* poll 57 per cent were "very or fairly confident" that he would *act effectively to tackle this issue*, compared to 47 per cent for Nick Clegg and 28 per cent for the Gordon Brown. The ICM-*Guardian* poll found that voters thought he had handled the issue well by a 20-point margin, while Mr Clegg had done so badly by 2 points (though with a quarter saying "don't know") and Mr Brown judged to have done badly by a margin of 46 points.

David Cameron's action was quite ruthless, and he was consistently and openly impatient with any Conservative MP who suggested that the public or the media had overreacted. Some MPs grumbled that Mr Cameron had not done enough to stand up for them. But he understood that this would be a defining moment: it would have been a catastrophe for the Conservative leader to appear for an instant to side with MPs against the public. While his own standing was enhanced, the episode drew further attention to the discrepancy between the leader on the one hand and the party – represented by the old-guard grandees – on the other.

The wider Conservative Party, though, was bound to the crisis in voters' minds: not just because Tory MPs were associated with some of the most spectacular claims, or displayed

95   David Cameron speech, 12 May 2009.

the most magisterial public disdain for their constituents[96], but because the expenses scandal was a feature of Britain's tarnished political culture, of which the Conservative Party was inescapably a component.

The expenses scandal did not change the political landscape so much as provide a focal point for the discontent that was already well established. (For the rest of the parliament it remained the story most likely to be mentioned when focus groups were asked what recent political events they could recall.) When people said they wanted change, they did not just mean a different party of government. The abuse of expenses was an illustration and a symptom of the wider problem: that politicians were disconnected from the world of the voter, and went to Westminster to play games and pursue selfish ambition at public expense. If Labour suffered the most immediate damage, strategically the Opposition had the most to lose. The expenses scandal stoked voters' desire for change, while binding the Conservatives to the old order.

96   Anthony Steen: "I think I behaved, if I may say so, impeccably. I have done nothing criminal, that's the most awful thing, and do you know what it is about? Jealousy. I have got a very, very large house. Some people say it looks like Balmoral, but it's a merchant house of the 19th century. It's not particularly attractive, it just does me nicely and it's got room to actually plant a few trees... I still don't know what all the fuss is about... What right does the public have to interfere with my private life? None. Do you know what this reminds me of? An episode of *Coronation Street*." (*The World at One*, BBC Radio 4, 21 May 2009)

5 / **Targeting**

DESPITE ITS SHORTCOMINGS, the 2005 election campaign had left the Conservatives within striking distance of winning back several seats. Eighteen Labour and eight Liberal Democrat seats had majorities of less than 3 per cent, and a swing of only 1.6 per cent would deprive Labour of its overall majority.

But returning to government was quite a different proposition. Following the boundary review, there were 210 notional Conservative seats in the House of Commons. When John Bercow was elected Speaker, his constituency of Buckingham ceased to be a Conservative seat so this fell to 209. With 650 seats in the new House of Commons, 326 were needed for an overall majority. There would have to be 117 Conservative gains for a majority of one. A target seat campaign would not be a substitute for changing the party and fixing the brand – there was no magic bullet that would reach a few thousand key voters and give us a short cut into government. It could, though, make sure that for any given share of the vote we maximised the number of Conservative MPs in the House of Commons. The job was to deliver seat bang for brand buck.

Target seats

It fell to me and my team – principally Stephen Gilbert[97] and Gavin Barwell[98] – to devise a targeting strategy that would encompass more seats than we had won at an election for 80 years, without falling into the trap of spreading resources so thinly that none received any real benefit. The target list would not just comprise the 117 smallest majorities. For one thing, some seats would almost certainly fall to us unless there was actually a swing to

---

97   Appointed Political Secretary to the Prime Minister after the election
98   Elected the Member of Parliament for Croydon Central on 6 May 2010

Labour. And since the party was aiming for a working majority, the plan would have to take us further into Labour territory than the 117th most marginal. There were also some seats in which sitting Conservative MPs were vulnerable. The outcome of the election would be decided in around 130 constituencies across Britain.

We decided to divide seats according to their priority. Initially there were five categories: "Consolidation" seats were potentially vulnerable Conservative-held constituencies; "Best Placed To Win" seats were mostly new constituencies with a notional Conservative majority but no incumbent, or seats with a small Labour or Liberal Democrat majority that we could be fairly confident of overturning; "Development" seats were those we were unlikely to win but which could be brought into play next time around; and "Long Shots" were exactly that. In the middle, between Best Placed To Win and Development, were the "Battleground" seats. These would receive the bulk of our attention – professional time, national literature, and of course money. Ultimately we streamlined the seats into three categories – Best Placed To Win, Battleground and Development.

In terms of parliamentary maths, we planned on the basis of holding existing Conservative seats, winning Best Placed To Win and Battleground seats, and that anything on top of that was a bonus – not at all complacently, but as a set of working assumptions. On this basis, our initial Battleground list would not have won us the election. Given that the Conservative party had very little presence in many of the seats we needed to win, our plan was to build up our capacity and organisation and help to kick start local campaigns, and steadily move the battleground in a more ambitious direction over time.

To that end, we carried out twice yearly reviews to decide which seats could change category, and whether the battleground was pitched at the right level overall. As well as ensuring that our resources were in the right place at the right time, this system gave candidates an extra incentive to perform. Good progress in a Development seat could mean moving into the Battleground category, meaning more central support and a better chance of winning. Naturally some candidates were reluctant to be "promoted" to Best Placed To Win, despite the vote of confidence this implied, since much of the support they received would now be directed elsewhere. But the system did not encourage Battleground candidates to soft pedal – those who did not perform risked demotion to Development status.

This element of accountability was an essential part of the target seat strategy. Before receiving any financial support candidates submitted detailed campaign plans. I reviewed these with my team at CCHQ, and we allocated funds according to the quality of the plans and the target status of their seat. We also set quarterly performance targets on canvass returns, literature delivery and voter contact details collected; continued support was initially contingent upon candidates' performance against these targets.

In the autumn of 2007, once the prospect of an early general election had receded, we took the opportunity to restructure our nationwide campaigning operation completely. The Conservative Party's field team had traditionally been organised along geographical lines, but this regional structure was too cumbersome and inflexible. Very late in the 2005 campaign, for example, it became clear that the party was doing much better in certain types of constituencies, like Harlow and Crawley, than in other target seats. Unfortunately, this insight came too late for us to be able to capitalise on it, and we lost both seats – very similar in terms of demographics, but in different regions – by fewer than 100 votes. We needed a structure that was focused primarily around target seats, and that helped us to campaign according to the characteristics of a constituency, not just where it happened to be in the country.

We assembled twelve clusters of target seats: in New Towns, Seaside Towns, Inner London, Outer London, Thames Gateway, Central Midlands, West Midlands, East Pennines and West Pennines, each seat had a similar demographic profile. Liberal Democrat seats were a separate cluster, despite their wide variety and the fact that they were spread between Cornwall and Cumbria, because they needed a different campaigning approach to those where Labour were our main opponents. Target seats in Wales were also treated separately. (The campaign in Scotland was the responsibility of Scottish Central Office in Edinburgh.)

The final cluster was a Miscellaneous group of constituencies that simply did not match any others. The Brighton and Hove seats, for example, did not fit easily into the Seaside Towns cluster, the city's profile having little in common with those of Blackpool, Great Yarmouth, Dover or Waveney.

The next stage was to appoint a Battleground Director for each cluster. These senior campaign professionals were responsible for developing and delivering a campaign strategy for the seats in their cluster. Each Battleground Director had a team of Campaign Directors, each of whom worked with a handful of target seats to ensure the campaign was delivered on the ground. This often meant having to build up a local organisation almost from scratch. Some of the seats we needed to win had been lost not in 1997 but in 1992 or even earlier. In such places the Conservative Association would comprise a diehard remnant, admirable in their loyalty but in no position to mount a full-scale campaign.

Selecting candidates as early as possible was an important part of the strategy. We had seen from previous elections that the incumbency factor was significant, particularly for MPs in their first term, who often did better than their party nationally. For our candidates to compete, we needed to give them as much time as possible to build their profile and reputation. Once in place we encouraged each candidate to put together a campaign team of energetic and trusted individuals who would commit for the long haul. This was essential to keep their campaign on track without becoming bogged down in the administrative minutiae of local Associations and their laser-like focus on luncheons, raffles and coffee mornings (sometimes not as fundraising opportunities but apparently as ends in themselves). Attending monthly meetings of the campaign teams in their seats became an important part of Campaign Directors' jobs, ensuring that the hard graft of canvassing and delivering continued to grind on.

I should say at this stage, before I am accused of trying to claim the credit for other people's success, that my admiration for our parliamentary candidates knows no bounds. At our regular meetings I was continually struck by their relentless energy and dedication, their extraordinary capacity for work, and the seriousness with which they took what they regarded as the call to public service. Careers were put on hold, holidays were curtailed and quiet weekends became a distant memory as candidates applied themselves to the long haul of local campaigning – many for their second, or even their third general election.

Target voters

When I presented our poll findings to David Cameron early in his leadership he would often say yes, this was all very interesting, but where was our next five per cent coming from? It remained true that as we continued to address our negatives, so our standing in the polls would improve, but we needed a more systematic way of working out where, and at whom, we should be targeting our message. In particular we needed to reach people who had voted Labour or Liberal Democrat in 2005, were not sure who they would support next time, and might be persuaded to vote Conservative. But who were these people? Where did they live? What were they like? What did they do? What did they care about? What kind of houses did they live in? What did they read and watch on TV? What was their outlook on life?

For years, all the main political parties had used Mosaic, a remarkable classification system devised by Experian, that segments the population into 11 groups and 61 types. (Experian have since launched an updated version; there are now 67 types of household in the UK, and 115 types of person.) As well as its own colourful nomenclature (from the metropolitan Global Connections and City Adventurers to the Sprawling Subtopia and White Van Culture of the suburbs and the Greenbelt Guardians and Parochial Villagers of the countryside), Mosaic gives detailed information about practically every aspect of the lives of each type, who are identified by postcode.

Though conceived as a commercial marketing tool, Mosaic clearly has rich pickings for political parties that they have long appreciated. Messages on schools, for example, can be directed at types most likely to have children at home. But what we did not know, until we took the trouble to find out, was how each of these types leaned politically. It was possible to make a series of educated guesses on this front, but with little certainty – trying to divine political affiliation through social group or demographic characteristics, at least among the professional classes, has been a mug's game since at least 1992. Canvass information could help, but was too patchy to be the basis of a robust model.

We embarked upon a project to combine Mosaic with our own polling to identify which of the 61 types were likely to be solid supporters of one party or another and, crucially, which were most likely to be undecided but persuadable to vote Conservative. The mechanics were fairly straightforward. In addition to the standard voting intention question, our polls asked how likely people were to vote for each party on a 1-10 scale. This enabled us to identify people who had not fully decided, even if they had expressed a voting intention question: a Labour voter who put their likelihood of voting Labour at six out of ten but their chance of voting Tory at four was very much up for grabs. By asking for each respondent's postcode, enabling us to identify their Mosaic type, we were able, having completed a big enough poll sample to make the model robust, to work out which Mosaic types were most likely to be committed Conservatives, which were solidly Labour, and who were the undecided voters who should be the main targets for our campaign.

We had a robust model by February 2008, based on a sample of over 18,000 interviews. Each Mosaic type was allocated to one of five target tiers: Solid Conservative and Solid Labour had a much higher than average likelihood to be strong supporters of one party or another and few undecideds; Top Targets had an above average Conservative lead but a higher than average likelihood to be wavering between one party and another, and Tug of

War types were evenly divided between the Conservatives and Labour and included a very high proportion of undecideds. In many cases these were traditional Labour voters who had become disillusioned and were looking for an alternative, however tentatively, probably for the first time.

Though we were putting a lot of faith in the data, the results of the exercise felt intuitively right – the results did not suggest that well-off retirees were all committed socialists or that local authority tenants were disproportionately Tory. The fact that there were stark differences in voting intention between different types helped confirm that Mosaic was a useful classification for political as well as commercial purposes, describing real and distinct groups of people, and that this was therefore a potentially powerful project. Of course the model could not promise 100 per cent accuracy (not every elector in the Top Targets category would be an undecided potential Conservative) and there is no substitute for comprehensive and reliable canvass data in which you know how each named elector is planning to vote because they have told you in person. But as a guide to the types of people we were aiming at, both in the media "air war" and the literature "ground war", it was stronger than anything we, or any party, had had at our disposal before.

Battleground Directors were given gigantic spreadsheets detailing the Mosaic profile of every constituency, ward and polling district in their cluster. For the first time we knew not only where to focus local campaigning to reach particular types of people, but how to ensure we were consistently reaching the voters most likely to switch to us. One effect of this is that candidates in marginal seats ventured into parts of their constituencies that had been written off as "bad areas" by their local parties for years, but which were in fact home to thousands of people willing to give the Conservatives a hearing if only we would bother to talk to them.

The cost of the polling needed for our target voter classification, as well as the time needed to build up a big enough sample and do the necessary analysis, meant that it could not be reviewed every six months like the target seat list. However, it was refreshed twice during the parliament. Though there was some movement, with particular Mosaic types moving between target tiers, the overall picture and relative position of the different types remained fairly stable, again adding to our confidence that it was a robust model. In the second round, though, conducted in the summer of 2008, the general level of Conservative support had improved so much that too many Mosaic types now appeared to be solidly Conservative. With 20-point Conservative poll leads we had to allow for the likelihood that some of those telling pollsters they would vote Tory were doing so mostly in protest at the Labour government, and that even many of those who really did now intend to vote Conservative might yet get cold feet. Accordingly we introduced a new Reassurance category, between Solid Conservative and Top Targets, comprising mostly those who had moved up from Top Targets but, we judged, still needed regular communication from us to keep them on board. The final classification was produced in the summer of 2009.

I do not propose to reveal the full breakdown of Mosaic types and target tiers since this would amount to a free targeting handbook for our opponents, but it is interesting to note some individual examples. The "Middle Rung Families" type has all the classic hallmarks of the Middle England voters so assiduously (and successfully) courted by Tony Blair: middle income junior professionals in semi-detached houses, with children at school and strong roots in their local communities, who are particularly prevalent in marginal seats in the Midlands and the South. Having been Top Targets in our initial model they moved into the Reassurance tier in the final round, as did a number of other types in the middle-income suburban habitat. This chimed with our more general observation that Labour support was much quicker to dissipate where it had been almost entirely a function of Mr Blair's appeal, rather than any traditional loyalty to the party.

"New Urban Colonists" and "Original Suburbs" were a good illustration of how class and income have become an unreliable guide to political allegiance. Living respectively in gentrified urban areas and spacious interwar suburban houses around London, these types largely comprise affluent young professional couples and families who are ambitious, educated and well informed. They remained in the Top Target tier, their liberal values no doubt partly responsible for their reluctance to commit to the Conservatives more solidly, and indeed for their above-average tendency to vote Liberal Democrat.

The Tug of War tier was a revealing guide to recent political trends. "White Van Culture" is emblematic of the famous "C2" voters who lent their support to Mrs Thatcher in the 1980s and exercised the right to buy, but swung decisively back to Labour in 1997. Now our polling showed them to be looking for an alternative, and they were an important component of the swing to the Conservatives, particularly in the New Towns and the Thames Gateway.

'Affluent Blue Collar' represents older manufacturing workers, who were found particularly in target seats in the Midlands and the North. Traditional working class values remain strong in these communities and Labour support would once have been solid. Yet from the beginning of the target voter project we consistently found that they were disillusioned with Labour and willing to give us a hearing (no doubt to their own astonishment in many cases). Our canvass returns showed that they did in fact come to the Conservatives in considerable numbers, helping to deliver our gains in the Central Midlands and East and West Pennines clusters, as they had in the Crewe & Nantwich by-election in 2008.

To some, the whole business of targeting in this way might sound rather cynical: instead of setting out our vision to the country as a whole we apparently cared only about certain types of people in certain places. Were we not taking probable Conservative voters for granted, and writing off probable Labour voters? And since most people live in one of the 500 or so "safe" constituencies that are nobody's targets, were we not ignoring the majority of the electorate altogether?

First of all, the target seats operation was just one element of the Conservative campaign, albeit an important one. Our strategy was a supplement to the national campaign that was taking place in every region and constituency in the country. It is also important to draw the distinction between designing a campaign and preparing a programme for government. The Shadow Cabinet and their advisers were working on every conceivable area of policy, not just those that would appeal to our target voters. Indeed, a huge amount of thought and work went into policies, such as welfare reform, that were designed to bring most benefit to people who were far from the towns and suburbs of undecided Middle England, and probably did not vote at all.

My job, though, was about the election, not what happened after it. We were charged with producing a campaign to elect as many Conservative MPs as possible, and the reality is that all parties have to use their resources where they can make the most difference to the result. A Conservative government would be for everybody – but you have to win before you can serve.

It is sometimes argued, incidentally, that parties' preoccupation with swing voters and marginal seats is a function of the first-past-the-post electoral system, and that if the system were made more proportionate, election campaigns would treat voters all equally. I think that is an illusion. As long as constituencies exist, some will inevitably be more competitive than others, and the parties will focus on the ones they are most likely to gain or lose, whether under first-past-the-post, Alternative Vote or something else. Even under pure proportional representation, with no constituencies at all, parties would still focus on the types of voters that their polling tells them are most likely to switch. They would have to enthuse their own supporters too to maximise their vote share, but this would never be enough to win. The voters in the middle will always be the prize, however their votes are counted.

Aside from the targeting strategy and organisational advice, the biggest tangible contribution of the target seats operation to campaigns on the ground was literature. Between October 2007 and polling day, target seats received nearly 74 million centrally produced fliers, leaflets, postcards, surveys, newspapers and magazines, as well as material designed at CCHQ and provided to constituencies to be printed locally. This was in addition to literature that constituencies designed and produced for themselves. The literature was usually accompanied by advice on the most appropriate targets for distribution, though in practice local campaign teams became adept at combining the Mosaic model with information from their own constituency canvass returns to ensure the right pieces of paper landed on the right doormats.

The message in our target seat literature was relentlessly positive. Though the style would vary according to the type of publication, the content would focus heavily on Conservative proposals on the main policy areas, and always featured David Cameron, either in the form of an interview or a first-person article. Often projects such as newspapers would emphasise different stories in different clusters of target seats, and literature would often include localisable[99] pages for features on individual candidates and specific local issues. Sometimes these local elements would also be produced at the centre – on one occasion a team of three people produced 149 separate editions of a constituency newspaper in three and a half days.

Where we did mention the opposition, the tone would usually be more in sorrow than in anger. A classic example is the series of leaflets, first trialled in the successful Crewe & Nantwich by-election campaign, designed to highlight how traditional Labour voters had been let down by policies like the scrapping of the 10p tax rate, under the theme "Who would have thought a Labour government would…". In practically every case, a negative message was accompanied by a positive one to answer the voter's inevitable and reasonable question, "so what are you going to do about it?"

The Mosaic model was an essential part of the literature campaign, particularly for tactical projects. When the 10p tax band was abolished in the 2008 Budget, we used Mosaic

99   An ugly word but a useful concept

to identify the types of people most likely to be directly affected, and who fell within one of our target tiers. Battleground Directors pinpointed the polling districts where these people were likely to be found, and within a matter of days volunteers were delivering half a million leaflets explaining the effect of the Chancellor's decision and setting out Conservative plans to help with the rising cost of living.

HOW MUCH WILL YOU BE HIT BY GORDON BROWN'S 10p TAX CON?

Nursery nurses will pay £154 more per year. Bar staff will pay £67 more. Catering assistants will pay £161 more. **Retail cashiers** will pay £185 more. Sales assistants will pay £227 more. Library clerks will pay £203 more. **Hairdressers** will pay £198 more. Receptionists will pay £167 more. **Home carers** will pay £157 more. School secretaries will pay £140 more. Cleaners will pay £45 more. Cooks will pay £136 more. **Dental nurses** will pay £132 more. **Typists** will pay £110 more. Call centre operators will pay £103 more. Bakers will pay £89 more. Florists will pay £79 more. **Caretakers** will pay £78 more. **Veterinary nurses** will pay £128 more. Farm workers will pay £75 more. **Legal secretaries** will pay £71 more. Hospital porters will pay £56 more. Van drivers will pay £51 more. **Road sweepers** will pay £49 more. **Pub managers** will pay £48 more. **Security guards** will pay £21 more.

| ON 6 APRIL, LABOUR INCREASED TAX ON SOME OF THE LOWEST-PAID WORKERS. | THE GOVERNMENT HAS CONFIRMED THAT 5.3 MILLION FAMILIES WILL LOSE OUT. | ONE IN FIVE FAMILIES WILL BE WORSE OFF – BY ANYTHING UP TO £464. |

(Based on the Office for National Statistics *Annual Survey of Hours and Earnings 2007*)

MY MONEY IN SAFE HANDS KEEP THE COST OF LIVING DOWN AND PUT STABILITY FIRST

YOU CAN GET IT IF YOU REALLY WANT

Labour have over-spent and over-borrowed, and as a result the public finances are in a mess. That is why Gordon Brown is putting up taxes, and kicking people when they are down.

The Conservatives have specific proposals to help hard-working families:

- We will oppose Labour's plans to double the 10p tax rate.
- We will use direct democracy to control council tax bills. We will give power to the people, through local referendums, to stop large council tax rises.
- We will raise the threshold for inheritance tax, taking 98 per cent of family homes out of it altogether.
- We will abolish stamp duty, the tax on house purchases, for 9 out of 10 first-time buyers, helping people get onto the housing ladder.
- We will end the couple penalty in the tax credits system. Taxes and benefits should encourage families to stay together, but the current system actually pays couples to live apart.
- We will reform the administration of tax credits to make the system simpler and fairer.
- We will help people into jobs and cut benefits for those who won't work.

JOIN US AT CONSERVATIVES.COM

Conservative 10p tax leaflet, April 2008

Over the course of two and a half years our literature was concentrated in a total of around 200 constituencies, with a total electorate of some 14 million people. In practice most of our efforts were focused on our target voters, which must mean we delivered, on average, nearly seven centrally produced pieces of literature to every elector. Target voters living in core Battleground seats could have received even more – and that is excluding direct mail, and material produced locally.

The question is often asked: does any of this make any difference? The answer is that it can, depending on the message, the presentation and the consistency. Regular communication shows that a party is active in the local area and takes an interest in what is going on (in places where Conservatives had all but died out, this in itself was an important message). It can counter the accusation that "we never hear from them", or, as bad, "we only ever hear from them at elections" – you can't fatten the pig on market day, as the old campaigning adage has it. Literature can help to raise the profile of the individual candidate, an increasingly important factor as trust in parties declines, and associate both the candidate and the party with an important issue. Ideally the content will be presented in such a way that it can be fleetingly absorbed, in the worst case scenario, on its short journey from doormat to recycling bin, but we found that a surprising proportion of our output was actually read.

Central direct mail accounted for a bigger part of the Conservative campaign than at any previous general election. A complex and constantly evolving plan, based on Mosaic analysis and polling, ensured that as far as possible target voters heard from us about the policy areas they were most likely to be interested in; issues included pensions, crime, schools, the NHS, welfare reform, civil liberties, the environment, immigration, Europe, tax and National Insurance, the economy and jobs, and cleaning up politics. As well as personally addressed letters from David Cameron or William Hague the scheme included punchier postcards; magazines aimed at pensioners or families that covered a wider range of subjects in a friendly format, complete with su doku; and the innovative final week "Contract with the Conservative Party", which was delivered to nearly two million target voters in the days before polling day. The direct mail campaign embodied an important principle of the target seats operation, that of "pace and flexibility", as Stephen Gilbert's colleagues never tired of hearing him remind them. As well as being well planned and thought out, the campaign was flexible and responsive, allowing us to incorporate new ideas and take account of changes in the landscape at very short notice. The "contract" was one example, which the direct mail team put together midway through the campaign as a response to the need, particularly urgent after the first televised debate, to crystallise the Conservative message and the change we were offering.

Over 17 million pieces of mail were delivered to target voters in Battleground seats in the five months before polling day. Nearly two thirds of our direct mail output included some kind of survey, usually on the subject of whatever the letter was about, but always asking for voting intention, preference of Prime Minister, and whether there were any particular policy issues that they were concerned about. This was an essential and formidable part of the operation. During these weeks nearly a quarter of a million surveys were returned to CCHQ where data was captured and analysed. This exercise enabled us to cease troubling firm supporters or opponents while ensuring that others were added to appropriate future mailings, either about issues that concerned them or messages targeted particularly at, for example, undecided Liberal Democrat voters who preferred David Cameron to Gordon Brown. Crucially, it enabled us to identify and respond to target voters who were particularly concerned about immigration or Europe.

From Edward Timpson's first campaign newspaper of the Crewe & Nantwich by-election, May 2008

From Esther McVey's lifestyle magazine in Wirral West, January 2009

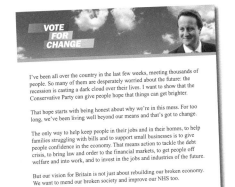

'Who would have thought that a Labour Government…' – with a positive message too.

Jake Berry's annual report to the voters of Rossendale & Darwen, November 2009

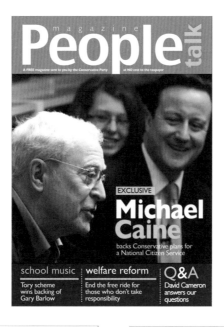

Magazine aimed at older voters, April 2010

Rebutting Labour scares, April 2010

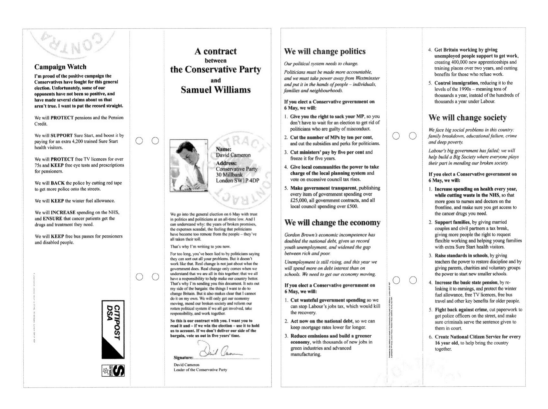

Personalised contract with the Conservative Party, posted to nearly 2 million target voters
in the final week of the campaign

FROM THE BEGINNING of the target seats campaign we treated Liberal Democrat-held seats, or seats where the Liberal Democrats were our main opponents, as a separate operation from other target seat clusters. Even though these constituencies were quite varied in character – seats like Cheltenham, Richmond Park and Carshalton & Wallington apparently had little in common with rural marginals in the West Country or Cumbria – they shared certain characteristics that required a distinct message and campaigning approach.

One feature of these seats was the overriding importance of localness. Liberal Democrat MPs and candidates have always cultivated a reputation as local champions and stressed local issues in their literature. This has often exasperated Conservatives. In 1990, Alan Clark wrote in his *Diaries*:

> The trouble is, once the Libs get stuck in, really stuck in, they are devilish hard to dislodge. Their trick is to degrade the whole standard of political debate. The nation, wide policy issues, the sweep of history – forget it. They can't even manage to discuss broad economic questions, as they don't understand the problems – never mind the answers. The Liberal technique is to force people to lower their sights, teeny little provincial problems about bus timetables, and street lighting and the grant for the new community hall.[100]

His complaint is completely futile, of course. The fact is that people do care about bus timetables and street lighting, and the thousand other small things that constitute community life. The Liberal Democrats had used this insight to great effect over many years, making their MPs (as the diarist observes) devilish hard to dislodge.

Apart from their local visibility, the most important appeal of the Liberal Democrats was simply that they were not the other two parties. We consistently found that the perception that Labour and the Conservatives spent their time fighting while the Liberal Democrats seemed more reasonable, or that someone other than the two main parties deserved a chance, were much more powerful drivers of Liberal Democrat support than national policies or personalities (indeed, for most of the parliament, we regularly found that only around half of Liberal Democrat voters could name their leader).

100   *Diaries*, Alan Clark, entry for 3 March 1990. Weidenfeld and Nicolson, 1993

This had important implications for the Conservative message in Liberal Democrat territory. It meant the campaign had to be relentlessly positive. Anything that came across as an attack, whether upon the Lib Dems or the government, was taken as confirmation of the sort of behaviour that put them off voting Conservative in the first place.[101] We also had to show that we had changed. We found that as with other non-Tories, Lib Dem voters' main concerns about the Conservative Party was that it would cut public services, that it would only look after the better off, and that behind David Cameron it had not really changed. In Liberal Democrat seats this mattered particularly because Labour's growing unpopularity would not be enough to drive votes to us. Many of these constituencies were once safe Conservative seats where people had abandoned the party for the Liberal Democrats in the 1990s (which also meant that Mosaic types who would be considered Solid Conservatives in Labour-held seats were not necessarily so on the Lib Dem battleground). Voting for an unchanged Conservative Party would have been no more attractive a prospect for these voters than it had been in 1997 or 2001, whatever their opinion of the Labour government.[102]

The pre-eminence of local issues in Liberal Democrat seats meant that our candidates, too, would have to be local heroes. This was not a sufficient condition to win, but it was a necessary one. If the general election in these constituencies was simply about who would be the best local MP, incumbents who had already established such a reputation would have an insurmountable advantage.

Two polls[103], conducted by YouGov for PoliticsHome, demonstrated this point. The polls were carried out in marginal seats and included two sets of voting intention questions. The standard question, *If there were a general election held tomorrow, which party would you*

---

101   This was quite frustrating for a number of Conservative candidates, since the Liberal Democrats themselves have no such compunction about going negative at a local level.

102   A powerful symbol of the "same old Tories" was any apparent preoccupation with Europe. Some have argued that the Conservatives failed to win several seats in 2010 because of the number of votes cast for UKIP. Their argument is that if the Conservatives had talked more about Europe and promised to hold a pointless retrospective referendum on the already ratified Lisbon Treaty (and, of course, given a higher profile to immigration), these seats would have been won. The number of votes we would have lost – not just in these seats but throughout the country – by appearing to have learned nothing from our three consecutive defeats seems not to occur to these people.

103   YouGov polls for PoliticsHome, 22 July-4 August 2008, sample 34,634; and 11-21 September 2009, sample 33,610

vote for?, pointed to a big swing to the Conservatives in both Labour and Liberal Democrat seats. The second question was as follows: *Thinking specifically about your own constituency and the candidates who are likely to stand there, which party's candidate do you think you will vote for in your own constituency at the next general election?* In Labour seats, there was little difference between the answers to these two questions, but with the Liberal Democrats the contrast was stark: in both polls, a string of seats that would be easy Conservative gains according to the standard question swung back to the Lib Dem incumbent when voters were prompted to think about their own constituency. The reason was very clear. The polls also asked voters to rate their local MPs on a number of attributes including *being a local person with roots in the area, being an ordinary person in touch with what ordinary people think and feel, being friendly and approachable for local people* and *keeping in touch with constituents through newsletters and leaflets*. Liberal Democrat MPs consistently trounced their Labour counterparts on these measures.

Our task, then, was to neutralise the local factor while emphasising the national: like the Liberal Democrats, the Conservatives could offer an excellent MP committed to the area; unlike the Liberal Democrats, we could also offer change for the whole country. This was not as straightforward a proposition as it may seem. It was far from clear to many voters in Liberal Democrat seats that the result in their constituency could help bring about a new government. The Lib Dems argued, somewhat mendaciously, that for Labour to lose the election Labour MPs had to lose their seats, and since there were no Labour MPs in Lib Dem constituencies by definition, the results here could make no difference. Though nonsense (because the more Conservatives were elected, the more chance that there would be a new government, whichever constituencies elected them), the Liberal Democrat argument had a certain plausibility, at least at first glance, for people who are not immersed in politics – which is to say, most people.

At the end of 2009, every elector in several Lib Dem-held target seats received a letter from David Cameron setting out our argument as clearly as we could: nobody was very surprised at the result of recent elections, but this time there is a chance to change the government; whatever the polls say, the result is not a foregone conclusion; to change the government we have to win the constituency you live in; Liberal Democrat MPs may do a good job locally, but at this election a vote for the Lib Dems is a vote to keep Gordon Brown and Labour in office; if you vote Conservative you can have both an excellent local MP and a new government offering change.

Once the election was called and polls suggested that the Conservatives would be short of an overall majority, discussion of a hung parliament climbed the agenda. A clutch of surveys gave varying accounts of how the public viewed this prospect, but we found the overriding response was one of confusion. Though people often said they liked the idea of no party having an overall majority, many had in fact never heard the term hung parliament and had no idea what it meant. Even more were puzzled about what it would mean in practice.

The idea that the risk of a hung parliament meant that a vote for the Liberal Democrats was effectively a vote for Gordon Brown was not readily accepted, or even understood. The argument assumes a degree of understanding about how parliament works that most voters simply do not have. As far as most people were concerned, a vote for the Liberal Democrats was exactly that. Why on earth did it make a Labour government more likely? Since the concept of a hung parliament was difficult and unfamiliar to start with, arguments about its hypothetical consequences were impenetrable for many people. Most had simply never thought about these things before. Why would they have done?

A second problem with the "vote Lib Dem, get Labour" argument was its inherent assumption that getting rid of Gordon Brown was the most important consideration for potential Liberal Democrat voters, and that they would prefer a Conservative government instead. But none of this could be taken for granted. For one thing, the inclination of Lib Dem-leaning voters to see elections primarily in local terms meant the repercussions in Westminster were secondary to the qualities of the candidates. For another thing, they still needed to hear more about our plans before reaching the stage of seeing a Conservative government as an obvious improvement. Moreover, many felt they had been let down by a long succession of governments of both parties: was it really a change to go back to the Conservatives?

In addition, people questioned the assumption that the Liberal Democrats would choose to prop up a Labour government in a hung parliament. Many felt that Nick Clegg would much prefer to deal with David Cameron than Gordon Brown (indeed there was a surprisingly widespread assumption that Mr Brown would not be troubling the scorer for much longer even if he won an outright majority). Even if a Labour-Liberal Democrat coalition were to be the outcome, at least Mr Brown would be balanced by the Liberal Democrats helping to make policy, and the Prime Minister would have a bigger squad to choose from when forming the new government. By the same token, in a coalition with David Cameron the Liberal Democrat presence would provide some reassurance for those

David Cameron MP
Leader of the Conservative Party

CHANGE IN HARROGATE & KNARESBOROUGH – AND IN WESTMINSTER

Nobody has been very surprised at the result of the last few general elections. If we are honest, Labour never looked like losing last time round, or the time before.

The general election in 2010 will be different. This time we will have a real chance to vote for change and elect a new government for our country.

But this won't happen automatically. Despite what the polls say, the result is not a foregone conclusion. For the Conservatives to form a government, we need to gain more seats in parliament than we have managed at an election for 80 years.

One of the seats we have to win is the one you live in: Harrogate & Knaresborough. Unless the Conservatives win here with Andrew Jones, we will not be able to change the government at Westminster – and that means five more years of Gordon Brown and Labour.

As you may know, Phil Willis, the current Liberal Democrat MP for Harrogate & Knaresborough, is retiring at the next election. I know he has been a popular and hard-working MP, and that many local people voted for him because he was doing a good job.

But at the next election, the truth is that a vote for the Liberal Democrats will be a vote to keep Gordon Brown and the Labour government in power.

The choice you face isn't to have either a good local MP or a change of government. Your local Conservative candidate, Andrew Jones, is dedicated to Harrogate & Knaresborough and will be an excellent MP. And by supporting him, you will be helping to bring about change for our whole country.

Like most people, Andrew and I think Britain needs change. We need to reduce our enormous national debt and get Britain working, tackle poverty and our broken society, strengthen family life, improve our health service, raise standards in schools, scrap ID cards, do more to protect our environment and clean up our political system.

We want to hear about your priorities too. The enclosed survey is a chance to tell us what you think about the local issues that affect Harrogate & Knaresborough, as well as the things you want to see a Conservative government deal with nationally. Please return the completed survey to Andrew and your local Conservatives in the envelope provided.

Remember – we need Andrew Jones as the Conservative MP in Harrogate & Knaresborough if we are going to change the government at Westminster.

Yours sincerely

David Cameron MP
Leader of the Conservative Party

PS. Your vote really will help decide the result of the next election. I hope you'll take the opportunity to vote for change.

Conservative Campaign Headquarters, 30 Millbank, London SW1P 4DP tel: 020 7222 9000 fax: 020 7222 1135

Promoted by Kate Mackenzie on behalf of Andrew Jones, both of Harrogate and Knaresborough Conservatives, 52 East Parade, Harrogate, HG1 5LQ & printed by DSICMM Group, Evolution House, Choats Road, Dagenham, Essex, RM9 6BF

Conservative direct mail, December 2009

still uncertain about the Conservative Party. Either way, a hung parliament held out the prospect of the Liberal Democrats serving in government – a repudiation of the traditional sneer that a ballot cast for the third party was a wasted vote, and an added inducement even for those whose decision was mainly local.

If the exhortation to avoid letting Gordon Brown return to Downing Street by the back door was ineffective, the message that a hung parliament was a bad thing in itself had slightly more resonance. We were up against two widely held views, which had begun to appear before the first televised debate. First, that such a result would force parties to compromise and work together for the good of the country, offering the best of the available manifestos and engendering a new spirit of co-operation. Second, that if it was change people wanted, then a coalition government in a hung parliament was unmistakably that.

An advertisement contrasting the hopes people said they had for a hung parliament with an alternative scenario of horse-trading and indecision did help to concentrate minds, not least because it chimed with people's rather cynical view of how politicians actually behaved (although, of course, the government now says that people's idealistic hopes have indeed become the reality). Ultimately, though, it became clear that although the possibility of a hung parliament was troubling for some voters, it was not in itself going to move many votes towards the Conservatives. The arguments were too full of confusing contingencies and hypotheticals, and in any case people did not want to make up their minds on the basis of something as remote from their lives as parliamentary maths. When it came down to it, you just had to vote for who you wanted to vote for and see what happened.

Half way through the campaign we judged that Nick Clegg's post-debate boost had put a number of Liberal Democrat seats out of our reach. Our intelligence told us that the party's stronger national presence, and the chance of Lib Dem MPs wielding real influence in a hung parliament, had solidified support, particularly for strong incumbents in what were already ambitious targets. At the same time, though, shifting patterns of support had created opportunities elsewhere, as disgruntled Labour voters moved towards the Liberal Democrats, bringing some previously comparatively safe Labour seats within our reach. As a result we diverted resources, including direct mail, to some tougher Labour constituencies. This mid-campaign redrawing of the battleground contributed to our victories in Amber Valley, Carlisle, Sherwood, Thurrock, and the gain that needed the biggest swing from Labour, Cannock Chase.

WHAT YOU THINK MIGHT HAPPEN IN A HUNG PARLIAMENT.

1. There will be a fresh new dawn in British politics.

2. There will be more open and democratic government with everyone co-operating for the national good.

3. There will be a new consensus of the best policies for Britain to get us through the recession.

4. Because of this new co-operation, there will be decisive change leading to greater confidence and renewed economic growth.

5. We will have found a new form of government which will break the old mould.

6. Hurray!

WHAT'S MORE LIKELY TO HAPPEN IN A HUNG PARLIAMENT.

1. Gordon Brown will still be Prime Minister.

2. The parties will get behind closed doors and horse-trade between each other over posts and power.

3. There will be haggling between politicians rather than any clear leadership.

4. This will bring delay and indecision leading to a drop in confidence, a fall in the pound and an increase in interest rates.

5. We will have to choose a new government in another General Election within a year.

6. Help!

Conservative hung parliament ad, April 2010

THE TARGET SEATS campaign began to attract attention almost from its inception. True to form, the press reported my involvement with varying degrees of accuracy. In July 2007 my team and I moved into Conservative Campaign Headquarters in Millbank (until then we had been based at an office nearby). I had begun to assemble my own political team during the previous parliament. After I became Deputy Chairman we worked closely with CCHQ, and it was always planned that we would become fully integrated into the party's structure – though I would still pay the team's salaries, declared to the Electoral Commission as contributions to the party.

To my amusement, our move from one part of SW1 to another was written up in some parts of the press as a portentous development. Peter Oborne described it in the *Daily Mail* as "something of a coup d'état inside the Tory campaign headquarters".[104] I had supposedly seized control over marginal seats, opinion polling and focus groups, and this had by his reckoning produced a sudden upheaval in the balance of power in the party hierarchy – although by the time we moved into Millbank these things had already been my

104   'Cameron, Lord A and a very Conservative coup', *Daily Mail*, 25 August 2007

responsibility for eighteen months. I often find that the small details in a story are the best guide to its reliability – in this case, the giveaway is the claim from an unnamed source that "[Ashcroft] has gone to the lengths of bringing in his own designer furniture". Anyone in a position to comment with authority on relationships at CCHQ would also have known that the furniture in my office was identical to everyone else's.

Some journalists in Conservative-leaning publications seemed mesmerised by the concept of Ashcroft-as-Blofeld, and it is indeed true that a member of the Shadow Cabinet was kind enough to send me a toy white Persian cat. The left, meanwhile, became increasingly (and gratifyingly) nervous about the possible effect of the target seats campaign itself, and started to grumble about it bitterly. Their argument was that devoting substantial resources to campaigning in target seats somehow constituted an unfair advantage. They also liked to say that the absence of spending limits outside election periods was a "loophole" in the law. But it wasn't, it was just the law, framed in Labour's own Political Parties and Electoral Registration Act 2000, and it applied to everyone. There was nothing to stop any other party doing exactly what we did – indeed that is exactly what they ought to have done. If Labour had decided, as we had, that the election would be won and lost in the marginal seats, it is baffling that they apparently never marshalled their own resources into a rival long-term targeting operation. Though they did ultimately put up a formidable fight in a number of constituencies, this had the feel of a series of heroic last-ditch stands, rather than a properly planned strategy.

Some Labour MPs – including Gordon Brown himself, who liked to mention me at Prime Minister's Questions when stuck for an answer to whatever he had been asked – became quite obsessed with the issue. Martin Linton, then the MP for Battersea, raised it in the House of Commons at Business Questions in October 2007:

> I am sure that my right hon. and learned Friend is as alarmed as I am by the sight of Lord Ashcroft roaming the country signing cheques for £25,000 at the drop of a business plan, for the few candidates who win his approval. Does that not smell of the Victorian era, when landowners controlled strings of rotten boroughs and could spend money to ensure that their candidates were elected.[105]

105   *Hansard*, 11 October 2007, col. 453

Harriet Harman, then Leader of the House, replied that "we should all be concerned that people do not like the idea that big money comes in and assists people in buying seats".

Phil Hope, then the MP for Corby, complained to the *Guardian* that "there's this un-level playing field where a millionaire can come parachuting in and see if they can buy the seat. It feels very American to me, and I don't think we want to import that kind of politics into this country."[106] Denis Macshane, the MP for Rotherham, wrote to the Speaker of the House of Lords in November 2007: "I doubt if there has ever been a single individual seeking by use of his own private money to take control of so many seats in the Commons ever in parliamentary history." Paul Flynn, then the Labour MP for Newport West, protested on his amusing blog that my "activities" were "scandalous and come close to cheating". Delightfully he continued: "He personally interviews candidates and selects the most mindless, raw meat-eating Tory loons... He ploughs cash into vulnerable constituencies in order to buy votes."[107]

Buying seats? Buying votes? This has always sounded an extraordinary argument to me. It hugely underestimates, even insults the intelligence of voters. Does Mr Flynn really have such scant regard for the people of Newport that he thinks they would elect a "mindless Tory loon" just because he could afford a flashy campaign? The same goes for the commentators who echoed this daft allegation. Do these high-minded individuals think their own votes could be "bought" in such a way? Of course not! Why do they think other people are so credulous?

The notion that more money means more votes not only does the electorate an injustice, it flies in the face of all the evidence. In the 1997 general election, and again in 2001, the Conservative Party spent roughly £2 million more than Labour[108]. Much good that did us. In 2005, Labour outspent us, albeit by only £87,376, but has it ever been suggested that that is the reason for their third consecutive victory? In 1997 the Referendum Party was reported to have spent £20 million on its campaign[109], compared to Labour's £26 million – yet not a single Referendum Party MP was elected.

106   'This is the frontline', *Guardian*, 5 November 2007

107   paulflynnmp.co.uk, 9 October 2007

108   Electoral Commission

109   *Independent*, 30 April 1997

The truth is that campaign funding only helps if you have a saleable message. If you are relevant and in touch, have a strong leader with a compelling vision and attractive policies you can be trusted to deliver, the more people hear from you, the better. If not, a lavishly financed campaign won't help in the slightest. Perhaps more to the point, if you are a good local MP in a governing party with a strong record, what would you have to fear from being opposed by a mindless loon, however well funded? Clearly, Labour MPs and their allies who complained about our operation were motivated by panic, not principle. Would they have been so worried if they believed in their hearts that Labour deserved to win?

At this time Sir Hayden Phillips was chairing the Inter-Party Talks on party funding, based on proposals he put to the representatives of the three main parties. These included a cap on individual donations, spending controls covering the whole of a Westminster electoral cycle, and proposed schemes for public funding of political parties. The intention was for reform of political funding to be carried out on the basis of consensus, not against a backdrop of partisan rancour. Even so, agitating by Labour MPs for the introduction of unilateral legislation to block our campaign gathered pace on the Labour benches.

Much of the case against our target seats strategy was based on a number of misconceptions (which, once I had set the record straight in an article in the *Telegraph*[110] and a letter in the *Guardian*[111], became deliberate misrepresentations). The first of these was that I paid for the whole operation myself. It was certainly no secret that I helped out and I was proud to do so, but most of my contributions were given in kind, in the form of seconded staff and polling projects. Indeed, a search of the Electoral Commission database – freely available to be examined by the public, including those who chose to misrepresent the position – will reveal that during David Cameron's leadership in opposition, cash donations from Bearwood amounted to £634,136.75. Not a pittance, but hardly the "Ashcroft millions" of popular myth. I was very far from being the only donor to the campaign; most of the money was given by others.

Next was the idea that I gave money directly to Conservative candidates or constituency associations in target seats. This was also untrue. My comparatively modest cash contributions went straight into the party's central pot. Candidates submitted campaign proposals to CCHQ, where they were considered by a committee, which allocated funds

110   'Labour wants to hamstring threatening Tories', *Telegraph,* 18 October 2007
111   'Why I donate to the Conservative cause', *Guardian,* 27 October 2007

to the ones we judged most likely to be successful. The idea that I grilled the candidates by myself and wrote a personal cheque to the lucky ones is beyond a caricature.

These two untruths, lazily perpetuated in countless articles at the time, were deliberately promoted to create the impression that I personally had an undue and sinister influence on the outcome of the election. The only real difference between my contributions and those of big donors to our opponents like Lord Sainsbury, who has given Labour nearly £13 million since 2002 according to the Electoral Commission, is that I have taken an active role in the campaign. For all we know, the Sainsbury millions may have been devoted to marginal seats – and if not, maybe they should have been.

My influence was in fact confined to the areas over which I had been asked to take responsibility, target seats and opinion research. I have never had, or sought, any say over policy, whether in my capacity as Deputy Chairman or as a donor. Here there is a stark contrast with the Labour Party, in which the trade unions' trading of donations for influence is part of the furniture. It is not just a matter of cash contributions, which have totalled more than £88 million since 2001, according to the Electoral Commission. After the 2005 election the Trade Union and Labour Party Liaison Organisation (TULO) claimed to have helped Labour to victory with, among other things, six million pieces of direct mail, including an average of 18,000 items in each of the top 100 marginal seats, and union offices were given over as phone banks to local constituency parties.[112] As TULO's website puts it:

> In affiliating to the Labour Party, trade unions get to play a major part in the Party's decision-making processes. This includes appointing members of the Party's executive, and its policy-forming body (the National Policy Forum) and sending delegates to its sovereign annual conference. Unions use all of these mechanisms to make sure that the Labour Party's policies reflect the interests of working people.[113]

Labour's biggest union supporter, Unite, was additionally rewarded for the £12.6 million[114] it gave to the party between 2007 and 2010 by the adoption of a number of its

---

112   *The TULO Strategy Delivered: How the Unions Helped Labour Win a Third Term*, TULO, 2005

113   'How we work together', unionstogether.org.uk

114   Electoral Commission

members and officials as Labour candidates in safe Labour constituencies – most notably Jack Dromey, the union's Deputy General Secretary, in Birmingham Erdington and John Cryer, one of its political officers, in Leyton & Wanstead. This exchange of money for policy clout simply does not happen in the Conservative Party.

The argument that by supporting Labour the unions are standing up for their members' interests is wearing increasingly thin. A poll of Unite members conducted by Populus[115] seven weeks before the general election found that their preferred Prime Minister was David Cameron (by 34 to 29 per cent over Gordon Brown); more than two thirds thought the Labour government was doing a bad job of representing the interests of ordinary working people in Britain; and 59 per cent disagreed with their union's decision to donate millions of pounds to the Labour Party.

AT THE HEART of Labour's disquiet over our targeting campaign was the idea that we now had an advantage in marginal constituencies. In fact we were struggling to keep up with the edge already enjoyed by incumbent MPs. It has long been the case that sitting MPs have a head start over their challengers. At the 2005 election, in Labour-held constituencies where the MP was standing down, the fall in support for the new Labour candidate was three times as big as it was in constituencies where the Labour MP was re-elected for a second term. Of course this may be partly due to the reputation an MP may deservedly establish through hard work and a high profile in the local media. But in recent years an MP's ability to make a name for himself in his constituency has been supported by a generous slice of public money.

In April 2007 the House of Commons introduced a taxpayer-funded Communications Allowance of £10,000 for each MP to spend on promoting himself to his constituents – though Conservative MPs voted against this proposal. In addition, MPs could transfer 10 per cent of their £90,505 staffing allowance to their communications budget, and spend £7,000 a year on postage.

On top of this they could help themselves to another £21,339 each in Incidental Expenses Provision (IEP), which could be used to cover constituency office costs, websites and other means of helping to get the message out. If they want to, MPs could transfer their entire IEP to their postage budget – meaning that they can each spend well over £40,000 a year of public money communicating with local voters.

115   Populus poll of Unite union members, 19-24 March 2010, sample 525

There could be few objections to MPs staying in touch with their constituents. But the effect of a glossy newsletter conveying a highly selective account of the Member's tireless work and glittering record, delivered free to every voter, will be to make it more likely that that Member will be re-elected – as, of course, it is intended to do. (How many Labour MPs do you suppose had columns in their spring 2008 newsletters headed "Why I Back Gordon's Scrapping of the 10p Tax Band"?)

Of course, Conservative MPs were entitled to these allowances too. But the cumulative effect of a scheme which makes it more likely that incumbent MPs would be re-elected was to benefit the party that had the most incumbent MPs: Labour. It meant that in the 100 most marginal Labour-held seats that would determine the outcome of the election, Labour MPs effectively had a £4 million a year head start, paid for from public funds.

In that context, complaining that the Conservative campaign amounted to an attempt to "buy" seats was absurd. If MPs could spend £40,000 a year of public money promoting themselves in their constituency, why shouldn't their opponents have done the same with money they had raised themselves? As Bernard Woolley might have put it in *Yes, Minister*, it's one of those irregular verbs: *I* keep my constituents informed, *you* are spending public money on a political campaign, *he* is trying to buy votes.

OUR OPPONENTS did what they could to whip up controversy and keep it in the public eye. In September 2008 the *Sunday Times* published a long article about donations to the Conservative Party by Bearwood Corporate Services, a company with which I was associated. Even though the piece made clear that "there is no suggestion that any laws have been broken", the Labour MP John Mann[116] felt that Bearwood's political donations merited a complaint to the Electoral Commission and a demand for a full investigation. I can understand why the Commission feels it must be seen to take complaints seriously, particularly if they are made by an MP. In this case, though, it did not distinguish itself. Although the complaint was without substance and was, transparently, a politically motivated attempt to tarnish my reputation and call into question the integrity of the Conservative Party's funding, the Electoral Commission somehow contrived (no doubt through ineptitude rather than malice) to string out its inquiry for nearly eighteen months in the run-up to the general election.

---

116   Who objected to our having the temerity to campaign in his marginal constituency of Bassetlaw. He held his seat at the election, and many congratulations to him.

During this time, not only did the Commission not ask to talk to the Directors of Bearwood, nor to me, it refused several requests for meetings which would have brought the matter to a swifter conclusion. Instead it wasted hundreds of thousands of pounds of taxpayers' money and distracted the attention of party officials who had to produce documents sufficient to fill a room. Meanwhile, for the duration of this wild goose chase, I was described in all media reports as "Lord Ashcroft, who is under investigation by the Electoral Commission". The Commission eventually judged, as the evidence bound them to do, that no rules had been broken. Mr Mann cannot seriously have expected any other verdict, but of course that was never the point: as far as "the Ashcroft affair" was concerned, the story was the story.

Labour were so pleased with this gambit – make an allegation, initiate an inquiry, and thereby create something that can be reported in dark tones as a "controversy" replete with "unanswered questions" – that they repeated it immediately. On 1 March 2010 I revealed in a statement that my tax status was that of a "non-dom", and disclosed the official undertakings I had given in respect of the award of my peerage ten years earlier: to become a "long term resident" of the UK and to resign as Belize's permanent representative to the United Nations. I also clarified my plans for the future:

> As for the future, while the non-dom status will continue for many people in business or public life, David Cameron has said that anyone sitting in the legislature – Lords or Commons – must be treated as resident and domiciled in the UK for tax purposes. I agree with this change and expect to be sitting in the House of Lords for many years to come.[117]

Three days later, on 4 March – the very day that the Electoral Commission published its report exonerating Bearwood – Tony Wright, Labour chairman of the Public Administration Select Committee, announced a one-off evidence session devoted entirely to me. This was an obviously partisan ploy designed to keep my tax affairs in the news for as long as possible – particularly the mistaken charge that I had undertaken to pay UK tax on my worldwide income – even though my statement and the release of the Cabinet Office papers should have put an end to the matter. Conservative committee members

117   'A statement from Lord Ashcroft', 1 March 2010. See lordashcroft.com.

and witnesses did not dignify this kangaroo court with their attendance.[118] No report or conclusions were ever published, perhaps because even this Labour-Lib Dem inquiry could find nothing substantive to convict me of. Again, though, the outcome was beside the point: this circus kept "the Ashcroft affair" in the papers for a few more weeks.

This sort of coverage obviously does not help, and I am sorry that our opponents' preoccupation with me created a distraction for the party. Disappointingly for my assailants, though, their efforts had little effect on the voters. The controversy was mentioned no more than a handful of times in focus groups, in passing, and never as a reason not to vote Conservative. In a *Times* poll[119] of marginal seats, when prompted with the story, 69 per cent said it made no real difference to their view of the Conservative Party (and those who had already said they were going to vote Labour and Liberal Democrat were by far the most likely to say the story made them less favourable to the Tories).

A number of our opponents featured me in their literature or otherwise tried to create a frenzy of local indignation at my supposedly malign influence, but to little avail. For example, Karen Gillard, the Liberal Democrat candidate for South East Cornwall, devoted half a page of one of her campaign newspapers to a picture of me; her doubtless puzzled constituents elected the Conservative Sheryll Murray instead. Gordon Prentice became quite fixated. In the 2009-10 parliamentary session nearly a third of his spoken interventions were about me, and his blog discusses me at endless length. Shortly before the election was called a reporter from the *Independent on Sunday* visited Mr Prentice's constituency to see what people made of the fuss he had tried to generate:

> "I don't know who's spending the money and I don't care." Joey Riley, a
> "recently unemployed" mechanic scratching a living in the Lancashire town
> of Nelson, is unmoved by the row over the amount being spent to win his

118   Two witnesses did appear: Sir Hayden Phillips, who had overseen the negotiations as Clerk of the Crown in Chancery, and Labour's Baroness Dean, formerly Brenda Dean, leader of the militant printers' union SOGAT. Baroness Dean had sat on the Honours Scrutiny Committee that considered my nomination in 1999 and 2000, along with Lord Thomson, the former Labour MP George Thomson. As I noted in *Dirty Politics Dirty Times*, some might think that for me to be judged by this pair was akin to jury tampering, despite the moderating influence on the committee of its third member, Lord Hurd.

119   Populus poll for *The Times*, 5-7 March 2010, sample 1,500

vote. "Is it against the law? Is it harming anybody? No. All I am interested in is who's going to help me get a new job, or promise not to cut my dole while I'm waiting to find one."[120]

Perhaps Mr Prentice's curious sense of priorities was one of the things the people of Pendle had in mind when they replaced him with the Conservative Andrew Stephenson. In any event, I wish him a happy retirement.

6 / **What happened and why**

THE EXIT POLL that flashed onto screens at the stroke of 10pm on election night predicted 307 Conservative seats, 255 Labour, 59 Liberal Democrats and 29 Others. It was greeted with something between scepticism and disbelief. A well-known blogger declared that he would run naked down Whitehall if the Liberal Democrat seat count turned out to be true. The dearth of Lib Dems was the focal point for the doubters: how could they have enjoyed the unprecedented phenomenon of Cleggmania, risen to second and even first place in the polls, and ended up with fewer MPs than they started with? Perhaps voting patterns this time had been so unusual as to confound the analysts. And if this number was wrong, the other numbers could be wrong too – including the disappointing Conservative tally.

In fact, of course, the poll proved to be extraordinarily accurate, and the pollsters, NOP and Ipsos MORI, deserved their plaudits. They overestimated the Conservatives by just one seat,[121] the Liberal Democrats by two and Others by one, and underestimated Labour by three. The Conservatives would indeed be the largest party in a hung parliament.

Across the country, the swing from Labour to the Conservatives was 4.9 per cent[122], and the swing from the Liberal Democrats to the Conservatives was 1.4 per cent. But with a final total of 306 seats, we did better than the changes in vote share alone would suggest. Thirty-two of the Conservative gains would not have been won on the average national swing: 23 of the seats we won from Labour required a swing of more than 4.9 per cent, and nine of our gains from the Liberal Democrats needed a swing of more than 1.4 per cent.

Without these seats, there would have been 274 Conservative MPs in the 2010 parliament. Labour would have been the largest party with 281 seats. The Liberal

---

121   Though for some reason best known to themselves, the BBC counted Buckingham as a "Con hold", taking the Conservative total to 307 in their calculations, when it is in fact the Speaker's seat.

122   *General Election 2010: Preliminary Analysis*, House of Commons Library Research Paper 10/36

Democrats would have won 66 seats. Labour and the Liberal Democrats would have had 347 seats between them – a parliamentary majority of 44. Instead, the Conservatives became the largest party with 48 more seats than Labour.

Constituency	Lab-Con swing needed	Lab-Con swing achieved
Amber Valley	6.27%	6.85%
Cannock Chase	10.50%	14.01%
Carlisle	6.73%	7.66%
Crewe & Nantwich	7.75%	13.67%
Dover	5.20%	10.43%
Elmet & Rothwell	5.71%	9.77%
Erewash	7.83%	10.45%
Gloucester	6.47%	8.86%
Ipswich	5.91%	8.12%
Keighley	5.24%	8.32%
Kingswood	6.88%	9.43%
Morecambe & Lunesdale	5.87%	6.87%
North Warwickshire	7.63%	7.69%
Norwich North	8.30%	12.88%
Plymouth Sutton & Devonport	5.56%	6.85%
Pudsey	5.87%	7.32%
Reading West	5.74%	12.05%
Sherwood	7.95%	8.17%
Stockton South	6.72%	7.05%
Thurrock	6.51%	6.61%
Warwick & Leamington	5.17%	8.76%
Waveney	6.00%	6.75%
Weaver Vale	7.01%	8.14%

23 Conservative gains from Labour that required a swing above the national average

Constituency	LD-Con swing needed	LD-Con swing achieved
Camborne & Redruth	5.13%	5.21%
Harrogate & Knaresborough	8.11%	9.09%
Montgomeryshire	11.40%	13.15%
Newton Abbot	5.25%	5.79%
Oxford West & Abingdon	6.71%	6.87%
Richmond Park	3.55%	7.03%
South East Cornwall	5.89%	9.13%
Truro & Falmouth	4.63%	5.07%
Winchester	6.37%	9.09%

9 Conservative gains from the Lib Dems that required a swing above the national average

This outperformance of the national swing was in marked contrast to the Conservative experience at recent general elections. In 2005, we beat the swing by just eight seats. In 2001 we underperformed by ten seats, and in 1997 we lost 24 more seats than would have been the case on a uniform swing.

Despite the clear evidence that the results in marginal seats made a decisive difference to the outcome of the election, some have concluded for various reasons that our target seats operation was in fact a failure. Professor John Curtice of Strathclyde University, for example, observed in the *Telegraph* that "for all the controversy that Lord Ashcroft's funding of the Tory effort in marginal seats has caused, in the event it seems to have made very little difference at all".[123] His evidence for this was that the average swing in seats where Labour was defending a majority of less than 20 per cent was, at 5.6 per cent, only slightly above that of the UK as a whole. Anne McElvoy mused in the *Evening Standard* on the day after polling day that if she were me, she "might wonder if this is all you get for your money".[124]

I would make two observations in response. First, in a close election a few percentage points on the swing in marginal seats can make a significant difference. Second, with due respect to the Professor, the measure of success for our target seats campaign is how well

123   *Daily Telegraph*, 8 May 2010
124   'So who's running the country now??', Anne McElvoy, *London Evening Standard*, 7 May 2010

we did in the seats we targeted, not in an arbitrary list. As I explained earlier, the selection of our target seats was not just a matter of adopting all those that needed a swing up to a certain point – it was rather more sophisticated than that. Our core targets included some seats that needed only a small swing but which we knew would prove to be very tough, and some that needed a much bigger swing but for various reasons – the demographic profile, or the absence of an incumbent – made them much better prospects. But even if we had selected our Battleground targets simply on the basis of the numbers, a swing only slightly above that of the country as a whole would not in itself indicate that the campaign was a failure. This would be to assume that the marginal seats campaign was the only variable, whereas, in practice, other parties campaign too. We needed to work harder for any given swing in the target seats than in other seats. This is why, in the North East for example, the safe Labour seat of Washington & Sunderland West saw an enormous Labour-Conservative swing of 11.6 per cent, while in the more competitive Sunderland Central we achieved a swing of just 4.8 per cent. In London, Justine Greening enjoyed an impressive swing of 9.9 per cent in Putney, but in neighbouring Tooting, heavily fortified by Labour troops, we managed only just over a third of that. Above all, Professor Curtice makes the mistake of assuming that the result would have been the same had it not been for the target seats campaign. Given the extremely tough fights we had on the ground, this seems an extraordinarily improbable assumption, even for an academic.

In our core target Battleground seats, where Labour were our main opponents we achieved an average swing of 6.27 per cent – an extra 1.28 per cent on top of the national swing. In the Battleground seats held by the Liberal Democrats, our swing from the Lib Dems was 2.98 per cent, again significantly above the national average (and despite the fact that, as Professor Curtice points out, there was actually a small swing from the Conservatives to the Lib Dems in seats where they were defending a majority of less than 10 per cent). We outperformed the national swing in nine of our 12 target seat clusters: East Pennines, West Pennines, Central Midlands, West Midlands, New Towns, Seaside Towns, Thames Gateway, Wales, and Miscellaneous South.

Some who question the effectiveness of the target seats campaign have focused on the seats we ought to have won on a uniform swing, but didn't. (This is rather perverse, given the much larger number that we ought not to have won, but did.) For example, Daniel Johnson declares in *Standpoint* magazine: "The strategy in marginal seats using Lord Ashcroft's money yielded disappointing results in some cases, such as Hammersmith and Westminster North."[125] Since he could equally have written that the strategy yielded outstanding results in some cases, such as Amber Valley and Harrogate & Knaresborough, Mr Johnson perhaps chose his evidence to suit his mood.

Even so, there are 13 seats we would have won on a uniform swing but did not (nine from Labour, four from the Liberal Democrats): Birmingham Edgbaston, Bradford West, Dumfries & Galloway, Eltham, Gedling, Halifax, Hammersmith, Westminster North, Wirral South, Cheltenham, Eastleigh, Somerton & Frome, and Westmorland & Lonsdale. In addition we lost three notionally Conservative seats – Solihull (which had become notionally Conservative after the boundary changes but had a Liberal Democrat incumbent), Eastbourne and Wells. It is worth asking why. Though there were a few individually disappointing and surprising results, we can identify a few common themes.

One of these is that the Labour vote held up unusually well in London. In the two London seats cited by Daniel Johnson as evidence against our target seat operation, Westminster North and Hammersmith, the Conservative vote share increased by well above the national average of 3.7 per cent. In both of these, Labour's share rose too, meaning the Conservative swing fell below the level required. And in all three of the London seats that would have fallen on the national swing (the other is Eltham, where the Conservative vote share also rose), the Liberal Democrat vote was heavily squeezed.

Another factor, which also helps to explain some London results, is that, overall, we did less well in constituencies with a higher ethnic minority population. In the seats we won from Labour, the average non-white population is around 6 per cent – well below the national average. In the twenty of Labour's 100 most marginal seats that we failed to win, the average non-white population is over 15 per cent – more than twice the national average. In the five of these seats that are in London, the average non-white population is 28 per cent.[126]

Wirral South was one of a number of seats we were disappointed not to win in the North West. There has been some suggestion that we were held back by the number of public sector voters, but this theory is not a consistent explanation – we managed a much bigger swing in Wales, for example, where the proportion of public sector workers is higher. (Indeed, the city in Britain with the highest proportion of public sector workers is Oxford,

125   'Talk is cheap: Now it's time for action', Daniel Johnson, *Standpoint*, June 2010
126   Figures compiled by Andrew Cooper of Populus

where we achieved one of our biggest swings against the Liberal Democrats, to gain Oxford West & Abingdon.) The evidence from our own intelligence is that the marginal seats in the North West region were among the most heavily targeted by Labour and the unions (in West Yorkshire, by contrast, a great deal of Labour activity seemed to be concentrated in Morley & Outwood in defence of Ed Balls). As elsewhere, the Labour campaign was dominated by scares about supposed Tory cuts, but leaflets and direct mail seem to have been particularly voluminous in this region.

On the UK national swing we should theoretically have taken Dumfries & Galloway, but in Scotland the swing was away from the Conservatives. While voting patterns north of the border are different, with the Scottish National Party the main rivals to Labour, this should not blind us to the fact that the Conservative brand in Scotland remains comprehensively broken and that there has been no Tory recovery to speak of there. Despite being staunchly unionist, as far as the Scots are concerned we remain a party for the English.

The result in Birmingham Edgbaston, which has also been the subject of a good deal of comment, can only be put down to Gisela Stuart, who is by all accounts an extremely good and popular MP. In the elections for Birmingham City Council held on the same day, compared to the 2005 general election result there was a 5.3 per cent swing to the Conservatives in the wards comprising the Edgbaston constituency, more than 10 times the swing in the parliamentary election. Ms Stuart polled 2,504 more votes than Labour local government candidates in her constituency, suggesting strong personal support. Popular incumbents help to explain several other results including Solihull, Somerton & Frome and Westmorland & Lonsdale, and localised difficulties for Conservative MPs help to account for Wells and Eastbourne.

But to answer Anne McElvoy's kind concern about the return on my investment, let me state quite clearly that I am happy. In the target seats our operation produced an above-average swing, an above-average increase in the Conservative vote share, and a string of Tory gains that would not otherwise have occurred,[127] and which tipped the overall result in our favour. That is what it was supposed to do, and did.

---

127   As David Miliband put it, "dozens of great Labour MPs were drowned in a tide of Ashcroft money" (*Guardian*, 12 August 2010). There was more to it than money, as I have explained, but I appreciate his endorsement.

I THINK the Conservative Party can be proud of what it achieved. We added nearly two million votes to our 2005 total, an increase of nearly 22 per cent, and gained more seats than at any election since 1931. That is not to say we could not have done even better. There is no point denying that we were disappointed not to win an overall majority. The Conservative vote share of 36 per cent was higher than in the previous three elections, but lower than in any other election since the war.[128] Yet in 2009 and much of 2008, nearly all published polls showed a double-digit Conservative lead, often in the high teens, and with a handful showing us ahead by 20 points or more. As Deputy Chairman I was a member of David Cameron's team and I am not about to start criticising other members of that team who worked so tirelessly to put him into Number 10. But it would be a pretty thin account of our campaign that did not offer some thoughts on why our result was not better than it was.

Plenty of advice has already been tendered on this question since the election, nearly all of it wrong. Two themes recur: that we were not robust enough in our criticism of Labour, and that by not putting immigration at the forefront of our campaign we missed out on crucial votes. Let me deal with these dangerous falsehoods in turn.

The charge that we let Labour off the hook by being too feeble in our attacks is made directly by Tim Montgomerie in his *General Election Review* on ConservativeHome. Tim's *Review* makes some fair points in other areas but this statement is mistaken both in its premise and its conclusion:

> Because the Conservatives didn't fight Brown with the same ferocity that Blair fought John Major, Labour survived electorally.[129]

Yes, Labour were negative in the run-up to the 1997 election, but the reason voters turned against the decaying Conservative government was not, as Tim claimed, that the opposition "endlessly, single-mindedly repeated the charges of sleaze, weakness and

---

128   *General Election 2010: Preliminary Analysis*, House of Commons Library Research Paper 10/36

129   *General Election Review*, conservativehome.com. I have the honour to be the majority owner of ConservativeHome. Just as I do not interfere editorially and Tim is free to write what he likes, so I am sure he will not mind my pointing out in my own pages when he is wrong!

incompetence" – people reached their conclusions about us from the evidence of their own eyes and ears, as William Hague acknowledged in his first party conference speech as Conservative leader in 1997.[130] Much more central to the outcome in 1997 was Tony Blair's ruthless determination to eliminate Labour's negatives. He set about changing his party, including scrapping Clause Four, despite inheriting a huge poll lead over the Conservatives on his election as leader. This, not his unsparing attacks on John Major, is the more useful lesson for Conservatives.

Tim complains that, because of a lack of Conservative ferocity, "voters remained confused about the degree to which Brown was responsible for the economic failure. He was allowed to portray himself at least half-convincingly as some kind of saviour in the banking crisis." There are two flawed assumptions here. First, that voters were looking to the Conservatives to enlighten them about the Prime Minister's culpability. They were not. Some believed Mr Brown was to blame. Many firmly believed he was not, either because it was a global crisis that originated with American banks, or that he had inherited the mess from Tony Blair (who had, perhaps, in typically crafty fashion, seen what was coming and absconded in the nick of time). Others were genuinely confused. Either way, Conservative politicians saying it was all Mr Brown's fault were hardly going to change their opinion. After all, the Tories would say that, wouldn't they?

The second mistake is that voters would only consider switching to us once they did blame Brown. In fact, plenty of voters thought, simultaneously, that the economy was in a terrible state, that this was not necessarily Mr Brown's fault, *and* that he may not be the best person to get us out of it. In other words, they were perfectly willing to consider voting Conservative even if they were "confused" about Mr Brown's responsibility for the crisis, or indeed if they were quite certain that he was not responsible for it at all. For these people, the missing part of the jigsaw was whether or not they thought the Conservatives would do a better job.

130   "I know why we lost. I am sure many of you do too. So let's not mince words. People thought we had lost touch with those we always claimed to represent. Our parliamentary party came to be seen as divided, arrogant, selfish and conceited. Our party as a whole was regarded as out of touch and irrelevant. That is the truth of it, and we have to come to terms with it." (8 October 1997) See also Gyles Brandreth's diary, *Breaking the Code*, which is a funny but toe-curling antidote to any suggestion that the public felt as they did about the 1992-97 government because of anything Labour said or did.

In a thoughtful reflection on his narrow defeat in Dudley North, the Conservative candidate Graeme Brown recalled an encounter that demonstrated why reinforcing the case against the Prime Minister would never be enough:

> I met a man in his late 30s in his driveway and I asked, of course, if he'd vote for me. He said he still wasn't sure – he was a disillusioned Labour voter who didn't want to vote for Gordon Brown – but, that, he "wasn't sure, with the economy as it was, that now was the time for a change". My heart sank at that point. We had just endured the worst recession in our history (with the West Midlands the worst affected region of the UK). Banks had collapsed under a regulatory regime established by the then current Prime Minister 13 years ago. Our budget deficit was massive and unsustainable, and entirely the fault of the government. (There are of course 20 other points all of us could make here about the Labour government's economic incompetence.) And yet at 6.30pm on election day, a relatively affluent middle class voter in Dudley was still weighing up if he'd be safer with Gordon Brown.[131]

This man clearly had no particular fondness for Gordon Brown, though he did not seem to hold him responsible for the crisis. Whether he could have been persuaded to do so is beside the point – his concern was the risk of switching to the Conservatives.

Since everything carries an opportunity cost, every minute we spent telling voters (to no effect) why they should blame Mr Brown was a minute we could have spent explaining why they should trust us. Worse still, negative messages were a barrier to people accepting or even registering the positive ones: we often found that people were so irritated by phrases like "Labour's debt crisis" and "Gordon Brown's recession" that they would often pay no further attention when they read or heard them, meaning they missed or at least discounted whatever positive statement of policy or intent might follow.

A perfect illustration is furnished by David Cameron's speech on "Rebuilding Trust In Politics" (of all things) at the University of East London on 8 February 2010. The speech contained many proposals on political reform that could have shown that we understood

---

131   'Why didn't we win the general election? Reflections on the campaign from the coalface of a Midlands marginal', Graeme Brown, conservativehome.com, 23 June 2010

people's frustrations and were offering real change. Unfortunately, it was briefed as a personal attack on Gordon Brown, so that is how the papers trailed it. According to *The Times:*

> David Cameron will try to turn the pressure back on Gordon Brown today with a stinging attack on his "secretive, power-hoarding, controlling" character. In one of his most personal attacks to date, the Tory leader will lambast the Prime Minister as a "shameless defender of the old elite". Mocking Mr Brown's claim to be a reformer, Mr Cameron will dismiss this week's Commons vote on a referendum on changing the electoral system as a "cynical attempt to save his own skin".[132]

And the *Telegraph:*

> [Mr Cameron] will say that Mr Brown is tolerating the "disgusting sight" of the Labour MPs attempting to use parliamentary privilege as a defence to serious charges… Mr Cameron believes Gordon Brown is to blame for failing to act decisively over the issue. In an angry and personal denunciation of the Prime Minister, Mr Cameron will use a speech on political reform to say Mr Brown is a "shameless defender" of the old order. He will accuse Mr Brown of proving that he "is just not capable" of dealing with the post-expenses reform that is necessary.[133]

And the *Daily Mail:*

> David Cameron will today attack the "disgusting sight" of MPs charged with expenses fraud trying to hide behind arcane parliamentary privilege rules to avoid prosecution… He will criticise Mr Brown for failing to reform parliament, adding: "Look how he tolerates the disgusting sight of Labour

132   'David Cameron gets personal with attack on "secretive" Gordon Brown', *The Times*, 8 February 2010.

133   'MPs' expenses: David Cameron will bring in law to stop privilege defence to expenses crimes', telegraph.co.uk, 7 February 2010

MPs taking parliamentary privilege – designed to help MPs fight for their constituents; for truth and justice – and abuse it in order to save their skins and avoid prosecution for fraud and wrongdoing."

In a highly personal attack on Mr Brown he will say: "He can't reform the institution because he is the institution – he made it. The character of this government – secretive, power-hoarding, controlling – is his character."[134]

And the *Express:*

David Cameron will today launch his most scathing attack yet on Gordon Brown over the MPs' expenses scandal. In a highly personal onslaught, the Tory leader will accuse the Prime Minister of "tolerating the disgusting sight" of Labour MPs attempting to use parliamentary privilege to escape prosecution.

He will also claim that Mr Brown's "dithering" and failure to take decisive action has made the scandal even worse, and brand him as a "shameless defender of the old elite".[135]

So much for "rebuilding trust in politics". We could have had a story associating the Conservatives with the kind of change people wanted. Instead, because of the decision to highlight the negative, we had a story about us doing exactly the kind of thing people wanted to change *from.*

A series of poll questions asked by Populus for *The Times* provided yet more evidence. Between February 2004 and October 2009[136] they regularly asked people whether they were *satisfied with the Labour government overall,* were *dissatisfied with the Labour government overall but I still prefer them to a Conservative government,* or if they were *dissatisfied with the Labour government overall and I would rather have a Conservative government.* Throughout the exercise they found an overall preference for a Labour

---

134 'Cameron's "disgust" over MPs hiding behind Bill of Rights', *Daily Mail*, 8 February 2010

135 'Cameron scorns PM "dithering"', *Express*, 8 February 2010

136 Populus polls for *The Times* – see Pre-Conservative Conference poll questions 2009, populus.co.uk, for data series

government, albeit by widely varying margins. Most importantly, though, among those who preferred a Labour government, there was nearly always a big majority for those who said they were dissatisfied with Labour but still preferred them to the Tories. There was always a substantial chunk of the electorate – between 25 and 35 per cent in the 2005 parliament – who did not need persuading that they ought to be dissatisfied with Labour, but did need persuading that they ought to prefer us instead.

The sheer pointlessness of attacking Gordon Brown was demonstrated once and for all in Rochdale on 28 April 2010, when he climbed into his car and, addressing not just his staff but his still-live lapel microphone and therefore the world, unburdened himself of the view that Mrs Gillian Duffy, the harmless pensioner to whom he had just been chatting, was a "bigoted woman". This excruciating incident mesmerised the media and dominated the news for a day and a half, yet it had absolutely no discernible impact on voting intention polls. This was because people had long since formed a judgment about Mr Brown. Those who had taken against him had either already decided not to vote for him, or that they would vote for him even though he was prone to behaving like this. His supporters, meanwhile, were inclined to be sympathetic to him and angry with the media for going on about it. (YouGov[137] found 77 per cent of Conservative voters of the stern view that it was "an important incident that said a lot about Gordon Brown's character", and 72 per cent of Labour supporters thinking it "a trivial incident blown out of proportion that will have no impact on the election".) If such a plain and incontrovertible demonstration of Mr Brown's flaws was not going to move any votes, why would Conservatives trying to point out his shortcomings from the sidelines make any difference?

The determination to press the case against Labour is one of the reasons, perhaps the main reason, why we had not reassured enough people by election day that the Conservative Party had changed and had their interests at heart. Greater "ferocity" in our attacks on the Prime Minister – if that were possible – would only have made this problem worse.

The argument that the Conservative campaign should have made more of the issue of immigration has been widely made, and I hope Tim will excuse my picking on his *General Election Review* again if I say that he puts the case more succinctly than most:

137   YouGov poll for the *Sunday Times*, 30 April-1 May 2010, sample 1,483

> The Tory silence on the electorate's second biggest issue, immigration, was like Manchester United leaving Wayne Rooney on the substitute's bench.[138]

There are all sorts of objections to this, but I will start with the evidence Tim himself uses to support it – a poll supposedly proving that "a tough policy on immigration was ten times as likely to win votes as lose votes". The poll in question was commissioned by Migration Watch.[139] It is always worth looking hard at any poll that seems to support the arguments of the people who commissioned it, and this is a case in point. The poll, conducted in Labour and Liberal Democrat held marginal seats, asked whether a policy of limiting net immigration to Britain to 50,000 a year would make people more likely to vote Conservative. This particular question came after seven previous questions on immigration, in whose preambles the respondents learned that "official figures showed that NET immigration in 2008 stood at about 160,000 people" and "according to official figures, the population of the UK will rise from 61 million today to around 70 million by 2029… According to official figures, around 70 per cent of that estimated increase – about 7 million people – is likely to be as a result of immigration." Not at all surprisingly, the poll then found strong support for a policy of cutting net migration. Apart from this problem of leading the witness, the question on whether proposing a 50,000 limit would make people more likely to vote Conservative (44 per cent) or less likely (5 per cent) is only of any use if we know which party these people already intended to vote for. Were these 44 per cent potential converts, or were most of them going to vote Conservative anyway? Almost certainly the latter – a guess which seems all the more likely in light of the fact that Migration Watch elected not to publish these particular figures.

Much of the commentary urging the Conservatives to focus on immigration relied upon polling evidence suggesting that it was among voters' top priorities. There is no doubt that immigration was important, but that is not to say it was an issue that would move votes in large numbers. The Migration Watch poll, for example, asked: "Thinking about important issues facing the country, which one issue, if any, do you think is most likely to influence your vote at the next general election?" But people do not, generally, decide how to vote on the basis of issues, let alone one single issue. In our own research

138   *General Election Review*, conservativehome.com

139   YouGov poll for Migration Watch, 6-8 January 2010, sample 1,524

we regularly asked people what they felt were the most important issues "for the country as a whole", and then "for me and my family", asking for three issues in each case. Using this more balanced and realistic measure, we consistently found that immigration scored much higher as a "country" issue than as a "family" issue, though rarely more than upper mid-table on either.

So, accepting that immigration was important to a large number of voters and very important to a few, the question was whether the Conservative Party needed to raise its profile on the issue. Here the answer was an emphatic no. Alongside our questions on the most important issues to voters, we asked what issues voters thought the Conservative Party most cared about. Consistently, we found that voters were more likely to say that immigration was important to us than they were to say it was important to them.

The Populus-*Times* poll conducted on 6 April, quoted earlier, asked which of the main parties was the most likely "to reduce the level of immigration into Britain". Fifty-three per cent said the Conservatives – a 39-point lead over Labour and a 44-point lead over the Liberal Democrats (both of whose supporters thought the Conservatives were the most likely to cut immigration). Yet in the same poll the Conservatives had only a 4-point lead on being most trusted to manage the economy, and were 3 points behind Labour on being most likely to improve the NHS. And at 39 per cent, they had only a 7-point lead in voting intention. Very clearly, then, if the lead on immigration was nearly six times the lead on voting intention, immigration could not be the key variable. Thinking the Tories were most likely to be tough on immigration was not, for most people, a good enough reason to vote Conservative. Talking more about immigration might just have persuaded even more voters to think we had the best policy on the issue, but it would not have brought in any more votes.

The following week, when Populus asked voters which party they thought had proposed that foreign workers employed in the public services should be required to speak English, 40 per cent said the Conservatives – more than twice the number who attributed it to Labour, whose proposal it actually was.[140]

If a high proportion of voters had said immigration was an important concern for them and their families, and thought the Conservative Party was less concerned about it than they were, and we were neck and neck with Labour as the best party to handle the issue,

140   Populus poll for *The Times*, 12 April 2010, sample 1,525

there would have been a strong case for a high-profile immigration campaign. But the reverse was true in every case. We were the most trusted party on immigration by a huge margin, and people were more likely to think it was a Conservative priority than they were to be concerned about it themselves.

These are reasons why a bigger focus on immigration was unnecessary, but in practice it would have been counterproductive. Not just because of the opportunity cost again, though this was important – every speech or leaflet about immigration is one that could have been about the economy or public services where our credentials were less firmly established. If the Conservative Party's big task over the course of the parliament had been to show that it had changed, then putting immigration back at centre stage, or anywhere close to centre stage, would have shown the opposite. The media would certainly have said so. We would have given the impression that we had reverted to a "core vote strategy", and this would have been taken as a sign of weakness and panic.

It was never the plan, though, to ignore immigration altogether. As part of his commentary, Tim says:

> By early 2010 the party realised its error and immigration messages became a big part of direct mail operations.

In fact, we had always planned to tackle immigration through direct mail, and this is what we did. Why take the unnecessary and dangerous step of making immigration part of the air war when we could identify, through local canvassing and survey returns, the very individuals who are concerned about the issue and undecided how to vote, and arrange for them to receive a personally addressed letter from David Cameron explaining exactly what we intended to do about it?[141]

SO IF THE problem was not a lack of ferocity or the neglect of immigration, what was it? What became of our apparently commanding mid-parliament position? To ask

---

141   Interestingly enough, this operation also demonstrated that immigration was not a big vote swinger. Arranging the name and address data for our immigration letters, we first identified all the electors flagged as being concerned about immigration. The next stage was to remove those who also said they were firm Conservatives. The numbers fell dramatically.

what happened to our 20-point lead is not, in fact, quite the right question: it is more instructive to consider why such leads were there in the first place. In June and July 2008 the Conservative vote share in published polls ranged from 41 to 49 per cent, producing leads of between 13 and 23 points. Yet this was overwhelmingly down to disaffection with Gordon Brown and Labour.

Floating voters felt angry and betrayed by Labour and, having been willing to give Gordon Brown a chance in his early days as Prime Minister, had concluded that he was not up to the job. They had a very bleak view of Britain and the direction in which they felt it was heading, were anxious about the rising cost of living, and felt that Labour no longer represented or even particularly cared about people like them.

Though their attitude to the Conservatives had become more positive in comparison, this was not because we had answered all their concerns about us. It was because in their dismay at the state of things, we were the only available vehicle for change. They still had no particular reason to expect that things would improve under a Conservative government, other than that they could hardly get any worse. Their concerns about the Tories had not gone away – for the time being, they had become irrelevant: things were such a shambles that change was needed at almost any cost.

So the answer to the question of what happened to our 20-point lead is that this was never a potential election result. We did not suddenly do something to frighten away voters and turn our double digit leads into single figures. Those leads were always soft, and it was always inevitable that as the election approached – and the pollsters' question, "if there were a general election tomorrow…" became more real – we would come under more scrutiny. By the time this scrutiny came we had not done enough to answer the concerns that people had about the changing Conservative Party – concerns that they had held throughout the parliament, even when putting us close to 50 per cent in the polls.

From the onset of the banking crisis in the autumn of 2008 to the beginning of 2010, most published polls had the Conservatives between 39 and 42 per cent. Given the prevailing view of Labour at the time and the strength of the mood for change, this should have been higher – and, as important, our support should also have been more solid. Throughout the parliament, a large proportion of those intending to vote Conservative said their choice was more against the Labour government than for the Conservative Party.

This was echoed in the early findings of the British Election Study, which found that notwithstanding the big poll fluctuations during the parliament, the proportion of voters who identified themselves as Conservatives (as distinct from intending to vote Conservative) immediately before the campaign was all but unchanged from the same period in 2005, rising from 24 to 25 per cent.[142]

In one respect this increased willingness to vote Conservative without identifying with the party reflected a significant improvement in brand perceptions since the 2005 election, when many people voted reluctantly for a Labour government they had no real wish to continue because they felt there was no acceptable alternative. At the same time, though, the softness of our support left us vulnerable to events.

Election year began on a positive note with the launch of the draft manifesto chapter on the NHS. Further draft chapters were launched in January and February on issues including families, mending the "broken society", ethics and accountability in politics, and reforming the public sector. The poster of David Cameron proclaiming "I'll cut the deficit, not the NHS", which became notorious for the supposed airbrushing of his image, was in fact a positive development – even people who had not properly taken in the message had at least registered that it was David Cameron talking about the NHS (and the alternative plan, another series of direct attacks on Gordon Brown, would have done nothing to improve our standing).

Yet towards the end of February, nervousness about our position in the polls culminated in a decision that by talking about our own plans – as voters had been pleading with us to do for years – we were drawing too much attention to ourselves. In fact, if one were to look at the list of Shadow Cabinet press releases from the beginning of January to the end of February, one would see that for every story leading on a positive statement there was at least one leading on an attack. Nevertheless, as George Osborne put it in an article in *The Times*:[143]

> Since the new year, we are the party that has been setting out the new policy ideas that will change Britain. Perhaps that has made it too easy for the Labour Party simply to attack us while escaping scrutiny itself. That will now change.

142   *Electoral Choice in Britain, 2010: Emerging Evidence from the BES*, Harold Clarke, David Sanders, Marianne Stewart, Paul Whiteley, 25 June 2010

143   'Blair was the phoney. We will be straight with people', George Osborne, *The Times*, 27 February 2010

I think the decision to focus on Labour at this stage was a disappointing turn of events. Since the cancelled election of 2007 there had been no enthusiasm at all for the Gordon Brown and the Labour government, let alone for the prospect of their return for another five years. As the election approached, the doubt that prevented voters coming to us was whether we would turn out to be any different or better. To show people that we would indeed be different and better should have been our guiding imperative until polling day. To argue that we should focus on Labour's record was to assume that there were voters who thought "I'm sure a Conservative government would do a good job; my only doubt is whether Labour deserve to lose". Few voters thought this.

This point was illustrated, surely unarguably, by a series of Populus polls for *The Times* on the question of change. Three months before the election, 82 per cent of voters agreed with the statement *It is time for change*.[144] Sixty per cent agreed strongly. Yet the proportion who said they intended to vote Conservative was 40 per cent. On the day the election was called, Populus asked a similar question intended to help get to the bottom of this.[145] More than three quarters thought it was time for a change from Labour, but more than half of these, and 41 per cent of all voters, felt *It seems like time for a change from Labour, but I am not sure that it is time for a change to the Conservatives.* Only just over a third (34 per cent) thought *It seems like time for a change from Labour and I think it is time for a change to the Conservatives.* This gap between the proportion wanting change and the proportion prepared to vote Conservative is the single most telling explanation of the election result.

Those who wanted change "from Labour" but not "to the Conservatives" were given various statements that might account for their reluctance and asked which they agreed with. No fewer than 80 per cent thought that *All the Conservatives seem to do is attack Labour, and that kind of negative politics is one of the things people want to change about Britain.* Nearly three quarters (72 per cent) agreed with the recurring theme *I'm not convinced that the Conservative Party puts ordinary people first.* A greater Conservative focus on Gordon Brown and Labour, then, would make the first of these problems worse while doing nothing whatever to help address the second.

There were two main reasons why voting Conservative did not necessarily follow from wanting change. First, many felt the sheer magnitude of the problems facing Britain

144   Populus poll for *The Times*, 5-7 February 2010, sample 1,502

145   Populus poll for *The Times*, 6 April 2010, sample 1,507

meant that nothing much would change whoever was elected. Second, most people did not feel the Conservative Party had shown clearly how it would do things differently: a Conservative government would be "a change", but not necessarily "change". Tory attacks on Labour, designed to clarify the choice, actually had the opposite effect as the dreary spectacle of political squabbling added to the impression that the parties were much the same. The posters featuring a grinning Gordon Brown and lines such as "I let 80,000 criminals out early – Vote for me" were by no means the worst example of a negative campaign, and at least had the merit of raising an occasional chuckle, but were nevertheless an expression of old politics which added to the impression that there was precious little real change on the horizon.

I wasn't going to anyway… but why should I vote Conservative?

Normal people, it is worth noting again, are completely mystified as to why politicians behave like this. Not only do they find negative point-scoring a pretty unedifying spectacle in itself, they wonder why parties don't realise how offputting people find it. The usual answer that is offered is that however much people complain about it, negative campaigning works. I doubt that this is as true as is sometimes claimed, particularly when the unpopularity of the opponent is already clear, for all the reasons I have explained. But much of the time I don't think the reason for attacking is even strategic. I think there are two more basic motivations. First, attacking is easier. It is very much less arduous, not to say more fun, to come up with pithy soundbites, press releases and poster copy decrying the wickedness of the other side than it is to put across your own plans in a succinct and appealing way. Second, politicians enjoy laying into the enemy. For all the talk of changing politics, from all sides, politicians love the game, and this is how the game has always been played.

In any event, the fact that we did not complete the transformation of the Conservative Party brand or establish ourselves as a party of real change had at least two major consequences for the general election campaign. First, it gave Labour's scaremongering about Tory plans more resonance than it would otherwise have had. Labour's scares were untruthful and often in very poor taste. Sometimes they stayed just on the right side of an outright lie, and sometimes they didn't bother. This is by no means an exhaustive list: a handwritten letter circulated in Bolton, purporting to be from a local nurse, claimed quite falsely that the Conservatives were planning to scrap a local maternity unit; postcards, some of which found their way to cancer sufferers, claimed that we would end the right to see a cancer specialist within two weeks (omitting to mention that the policy of allowing doctors to set clinical priorities would have meant patients actually being seen sooner than that); literature[146] stated that the Conservatives "could see tax credits restricted to families where both parents earn at most £16,000 each on average", a claim that was simply invented (the Conservative manifesto[147] was clear that we would "stop paying tax credits to better off families with incomes over £50,000"); a letter from Natascha Engel, then the MP for North East Derbyshire, warned pensioners that the Conservatives had "promised to cut the Pension Credit and scrap the Winter Fuel Allowance", which is as straightforward a lie as you will hear in politics or anywhere else; other Labour literature merely implied that we would remove these things without actually saying so.[148]

---

146 *A future fair for all…It's your choice*, Labour Party, p. 9

147 *Invitation to Join the Government of Britain*, Conservative manifesto 2010, p. 8

148 Some of these messages were delivered in rather a heavy-handed way. We have anecdotal reports of voters in the North West receiving telephone calls in which they are told that the caller will probably die of cancer if the Tories get in. We have further anecdotal reports of Labour street canvassers *letting themselves into people's houses* if they failed to answer the door, in order to persuade them to get out and vote.

Labour cancer scare postcards, March 2010:
"the Tories will *scrap* your right to see a cancer specialist within two weeks".

Swing voters usually took this sort of literature with a large pinch of salt, but most did not dismiss it out of hand. Some disillusioned Labour voters, while applying a heavy discount to the "propaganda", remained chary enough of Tory motives to think there was probably some truth in it somewhere. Conservative rebuttal statements setting the record straight were not hugely reassuring, and certainly not the final word on the matter – they was merely the other side of a party political argument in which neither side could really be trusted. To make sense of such a ding-dong, you just had to go with your instincts.

This is where brand is absolutely crucial. We found that rebuttals did work when they were put in terms like: "WE WILL KEEP the winter fuel allowance", not because the Tories would never try anything so terrible as to scrap it but because the statement was so unambiguous it would be impossible to go back on. Literature of this kind was produced to counter all the scares we became aware of, and some of the damage was mitigated. But if the work on changing underlying perceptions of the party had been finished, scares like this would not have worked in the first place. They would have been at odds with what people felt they knew about the Conservatives, just as, in 1997, attempts to portray New Labour as a high tax party yoked to Europe and the unions fell flat. As Shaun Bailey, our excellent but sadly defeated candidate in Hammersmith, put it: "We were not fighting the Labour Party, we were fighting their version of our past, of our history, and that was the problem. It's easy for them to terrify people about our past and what we'd do in the future, and that's why we didn't quite make it over the line."[149]

The Conservative brand, as seen from Glasgow (See third box down on the left)

The second and related consequence of the incomplete brand transformation was that, even for voters who had had more than enough of Labour in government, voting Conservative was a much harder decision to make than it might have been. In early 2010, we found that some people who still took a very dim view of the Conservative Party were starting to say – usually after a deep breath and a good deal of grimacing – that they would have to vote Tory because it was time for a change.[150] This decision was usually provisional and was taken without enthusiasm. Very often they would say their father or grandfather would be spinning in their grave if they knew they were even thinking about it. The poster campaign featuring members of the public who were supporting us despite having "Never voted Tory before", was designed to encourage exactly these people.

The idea of voting Conservative was a big step and sometimes a big risk, and they remained open to alternative routes to change if they could find one that looked realistic. This was reflected in polls at the beginning of the campaign: six days after Mr Brown went to the Palace, Populus[151] found a third of voters saying their preferred result would be a hung parliament, compared to only 28 per cent who preferred a Conservative majority. This helps to explain a small but measurable uptick in Liberal Democrat support, from an average of around 18.5 per cent in the first week of April to around 21 per cent in the second week. An ICM poll for the *Sunday Telegraph,* conducted over the two nights before the first televised leaders' debate, put the party on 27 per cent.

This trickle became a flood after the first debate in Manchester on 15 April, when Cleggmania was visited upon us. Four polls of viewers conducted by Populus, YouGov, ComRes and Angus Reid all found Mr Clegg the clear winner. On the day of the debate, the YouGov-*Sun* daily tracking poll of voting intention had the Liberal Democrats third on 22 per cent; the following day they were in second place on 30 per cent and by Monday they were in the lead on 33 per cent.

Mr Clegg's appeal was more than sheer novelty. He had articulated a very widely held frustration with mainstream politics, and with his straightforward answers on

---

150   The fact that they reached this judgment, however reluctantly, is not a vindication of the decision to focus much of the campaign on attacking Labour – the feeling that they were voting for rather than just against something would have made the decision easier, and would have meant more people making it. At best, negative votes alone would have amounted to a pretty meagre and grudging majority.

151   Populus poll for *The Times*, 12 April 2010, sample 1,525

policy questions seemed to embody the possibility of real change – more than people had previously realised was on offer. Moreover, for many voters he had given his party a credibility that it had previously lacked.

This was clearly going to be much more of a problem for the Conservatives than for Labour. Much of the remaining Labour vote was either too tribal to contemplate switching, or preferred "the devil you know" to "change". We were competing with the Liberal Democrats for the "change" vote, so the large chunk of our own support that was motivated only by the desire to get rid of Labour, rather than any positive view of the Conservative Party, was vulnerable. Our attempts to frame the election as a straight choice between Labour and the Conservatives – and our billboards attacking Gordon Brown – suddenly looked very last season.

After the first debate the Liberal Democrats' average poll rating rocketed from just over 20 per cent to just over 30 per cent. Their share drifted back down by around 3 points by the final week of the campaign. On the day, they achieved only 23.6 per cent of the vote – better than where they started, but nowhere near their mid-campaign peak. In their final eve-of-election polls, every company overestimated the Liberal Democrat vote share – by between 2 points (ICM) and 5 points (Angus Reid and TNS BMRB).[152]

	Conservative	Labour	Liberal Democrat
6 April to First debate	39.38%	32.0%	20.85%
First debate to Second debate	32.39%	26.72%	30.39%
Second debate to Third debate	34.11%	27.68%	28.79%
Third debate to 6 May	35.06%	27.59%	27.53%
RESULT	36.9%	29.7%	23.6%

Average poll ratings cf. election result (Great Britain)[153]

There are two possibilities. Either the polls overestimated the Liberal Democrats' vote share and the party's apparent boost in support was illusory, or significant numbers

152   'An early post-mortem', Anthony Wells, *UK Polling Report*, 7 May 2010
153   Data compiled by Populus

of people who really did intend to vote for them changed their minds at the very end of the campaign.

There is evidence for both. In the campaign polls, Liberal Democrat support was disproportionately drawn from groups who are the least likely to turn out and vote: young people, and people who did not vote in 2005. The dilemma for pollsters here is how to deal with a 25 year-old who did not vote at the last election but insists he will turn out this time, when the evidence is that he may well not (although the phenomenon of a suddenly popular politician is not one that is likely to trouble them too often). It is also possible that, although poll samples are random and representative, people are more likely to agree to take part if they have at least a passing interest in politics. These people were more likely to have watched one or more of the debates and paid some attention to the election coverage, and may therefore have been more susceptible to Cleggmania.

After the election, ICM tried to shed some light on the question by conducting a "call-back" survey, re-contacting voters they had polled during the campaign. In a subsequent paper for *Research*, Martin Boon and John Curtice concluded that the main problem was voters who had declined to admit during the campaign that they planned to vote Labour. One in five of those who actually voted failed to declare their voting intention in ICM's final campaign poll, and they were nearly twice as likely to vote Labour as Liberal Democrat. A late swing could only account for a small part of the apparent overestimate of the Lib Dem vote share: 87 per cent of those who said they intended to vote for the party actually did so (though of course we only have those voters' words for that), not far behind the 95 per cent of Conservatives and 93 per cent of Labour voters casting their ballots as they said they would. Those who switched to the Liberal Democrats at the last minute almost equalled those who defected.[154]

It does seem likely, though, that a late swing away from the Liberal Democrats did play some part. After all, in the campaign polls, Liberal Democrat voters were consistently more likely to say they might change their mind and vote for another party than were Conservative or Labour supporters. There is some anecdotal evidence, that tallies of postal votes – which could have been cast a week or more before polling day – bore more resemblance to the final polls than the final result.[155] Many of those who decided on

---

154   'General Election 2010: Did the opinion polls flatter to deceive?', *Research*, 6 July 2010.

155   E.g. see 'Were the postal voters indicating that the polls were right?', Mike Smithson, politicalbetting.com, 24 May 2010.

the day, in other words, had a change of heart and turned back to the two main parties. We also have reports that some Labour voters who had decided to switch to the Lib Dems moved back again at the very last minute, for fear that their party would not just be defeated but wiped out.

Populus found some evidence for a last-minute shift in their final poll. In their fieldwork conducted on Tuesday 4 May, the Lib Dems were at 29 per cent, but in the interviews conducted on the eve of election day they dropped to 24 per cent.[156] Confusingly, though, this was not true for all pollsters. IpsosMORI conducted all the fieldwork for their final poll on the Wednesday, and put the Liberal Democrats on 27 per cent. In their post-election poll for the *News of the World*, 28 per cent claimed to have voted for the party – suggesting a consistent overestimation rather than a drop-off in support.[157] Overall it seems likely that some voters did turn away from the Liberal Democrats when it came to the crunch, but that this is not enough to account for the discrepancy between the polls and their final vote share.

Another question related to the reliability of the Lib Dem poll share is this: how much impact did the television debates really have on the outcome of the election? Daniel Finkelstein of *The Times* noted in December 2009[158] that studies had shown their effect in America to be fairly limited, with margins of victory already largely set before the debates start. The reasons for the lack of impact in the US were that debates often have no clear winner on the night, according to polls of viewers; that they happen too late in the campaign to have much impact since the important events have already happened; and that most viewers are partisans rooting for one side or the other.

Arguably, though, none of these things was true of our debates: polls found that Nick Clegg clearly won the first round, and David Cameron the third; the debates were the only events of the campaign to make any real impact on the voters[159]; and the viewers were far from being committed to one side or the other – by the time of the debates there was no shortage of swing voters who had not settled on a decision. Indeed, according to

---

156   Andrew Cooper, 'How the polls really got it right', *The Times Guide to the House of Commons 2010*, p. 31

157   Ipsos MORI poll for the *News of the World*, 12-13 May 2010, sample 1,023; see also 'What went wrong', Anthony Wells, *UK Polling Report*, 21 May 2010

158   'TV debates: Do they matter?', *Comment Central*, timesonline.co.uk, 22 December 2009

159   The only other notable campaign event, 'bigotgate', did not sway any votes. See above.

Ipsos MORI, 28 per cent of voters did not decide how to vote until the last week of the campaign[160], compared to only 19 per cent in 2005 and only 14 per cent in 2001. It is true that the Lib Dems' vote share was closer to their pre-debate poll rating than their numbers during the campaign: in the few days before the first debate, most polls put the party in the low 20s – very close to what they ultimately achieved. But there is an alternative to the interpretation that the debates did not matter: that without them, the Liberal Democrats would have done even worse than they did. It is impossible to know whether or not this is true, since there is no parallel universe in which the debates did not happen (at least, not one from which data are readily available).

What we know for sure is that the debates changed the narrative and the rhythm of the campaign.[161] They gave the momentum and the spotlight to the Liberal Democrats during crucial weeks when David Cameron had been hoping finally to seal the deal, and brought Nick Clegg to a new and appreciative audience.[162] Some of the effect may have been mitigated by David Cameron's victory in the final contest[163], the closer scrutiny of Liberal Democrat policies like not replacing Trident and an amnesty for illegal immigrants, and, at the margins, some reaction against the possibility of a hung parliament. But over those weeks, much of the limited attention that people have to spare for politics had been diverted to the Liberal Democrats and away from the Conservatives.

In an election night interview[164] with Andrew Neil, I said that the televised leaders' debates had changed the playing field, and that, to take "a pure, strategic hindsight view", had probably contributed to the narrowing of the Conservative lead. When the idea of a three-way debate was first mooted I warned that I thought this was a risk. I had two concerns. First was the precedent of the 1992 presidential election in the United States. The independent candidate Ross Perot had been polling at around 10 per cent in the week before the first televised debate on 11 October, in which he participated with President Bush

160   Ipsos MORI poll, 13 May 2010, sample 745

161   As Peter Mandelson also noted in his memoir, *The Third Man: Life at the Heart of New Labour*

162   As Daniel Finkelstein had also suggested in his December 2009 post, "but perhaps the debates will prove the equivalent of a convention for Nick Clegg".

163   According to all five published polls: Populus, ICM, YouGov, ComRes, ICM, 29 April 2010

164   MAA interview with Andrew Neil, BBC election night programme, 7 May 2010

and Bill Clinton.[165] Following his strong performance his numbers climbed and he won 19 per cent of the popular vote on 3 November.

I was also worried about the effect on the campaign in the target seats. In the research prior to the 2005 election, recorded in *Smell the Coffee*,[166] we discovered just how hard it is to convey a political message in a way that the public hear and absorb. I recorded how few people could recall anything at all when asked *Has there been anything in the news about what the Conservative Party has been saying or doing that has caught your eye this week, whether on TV or radio or in the papers?* Reviewing the data again I find that in 113 days of tracking, the average proportion of respondents answering "nothing" to that question was 77 per cent. On the record days for recall – 24 to 27 January, more than three months before the election – only 38 per cent could remember anything at all (of which 31 per cent mentioned immigration and 6 per cent mentioned tax cuts). This was an important part of the reason for building a concerted doorstep campaign in the target seats: since reaching people with a clear message in the media was so hard, we would have to do it quite literally on foot. We needed to select candidates early, identify key voters and communicate with them consistently, and this is what we had done. The prospect of televised debates – probably the only events of the campaign that had the potential to compel the attention of these voters – meant jeopardising years of steady campaigning on one roll (or three rolls) of the dice.

I was not responsible for our party's communications and nor did I want to be, so I do not hold the decision to go ahead with the debates against those who took it or advised it. After all, the arguments in favour were attractive too: David Cameron was our biggest asset, so the more people saw of him the better; he would shine, especially in comparison to Gordon Brown, making the choice of Prime Ministers clearer than ever; and he would have a perfect chance to answer the doubts people still had about what a Conservative government would actually do (indeed, each of these arguments was vindicated by the third debate). Given his consistent support for televised prime ministerial debates since the time of the leadership election, it would have been difficult to pull out once it became clear Gordon Brown was game. And on the question of the third party threat – well, with due respect to Mr Clegg, he had never given us much reason to suppose that he was capable of taking the country by storm.

165　'Despite Perot's re-entry, Clinton retains big lead', *New York Times*, 7 October 1992
166　*Smell the Coffee: A Wake-Up Call for the Conservative Party*, June 2005, pp. 33-40, 57, 70-72

Nevertheless, in an election where voters contemplated the prospect of a real change of government for the first time in 13 years, the debates helped the third party to maintain its profile and prevent itself becoming squeezed any further than it was. Voters who had been reluctantly concluding that they were going to have to grit their teeth and vote Conservative now found that the more palatable alternative was now also more credible than they had previously thought.

As with the Labour scares, though, the debates were not what deprived us of a majority. They were, perhaps, a tactical error that exposed a strategic problem: their impact would have been much less if we had already been where we should have been in the public mind. The problem was that three weeks before the general election the market was still wide open for a party of change. Nick Clegg was only able to appropriate the territory of "real change" because we did not dominate it ourselves.

***

The purpose of this book has been to explore the reasons why the Conservative Party ended up with 306 seats at the 2010 general election – no fewer, but no more. Given where the party started from, it was an historic achievement – but nobody would deny that until the very final stages of the campaign, we hoped and expected to do better. Looking at both sides of the equation, let me sum up the reasons as I see them.

WHY DID WE win two million more votes than in 2005, become the largest party in the House of Commons, gain more seats than at any election for 80 years and return to government having suffered three disastrous defeats in a row? Because David Cameron smelt the coffee. He recognised the need to change the Conservative Party, both in reality and in the eyes of the voters, and he did so. The fact that there is more to do on this front does not take away from what he has achieved. He ensured our candidates became more like the electorate we were asking to vote for them. He presented the party in a new way, capturing the media's attention with unusual visits like the much-mocked but successful "hug-a-husky" trip. He associated the Conservatives with a new agenda that made people look at us again. He campaigned on the NHS, giving the party credibility on the issue and ensuring it was no longer one on which Labour enjoyed a runaway lead. He resisted demands to push immigration back up the Conservative agenda. With George Osborne, he maintained a measured approach to the economy, refusing early calls for a promise of upfront tax cuts that would have shattered our credibility as the deficit deepened. He responded immediately and decisively to the expenses scandal, grasping the public mood and dealing ruthlessly with offenders.

A striking thing about this list of achievements is that each and every one of them was accomplished in the teeth of furious opposition from supposedly Conservative-supporting bloggers, commentators, newspapers and even some Tory MPs. These people now like to say the modernisation agenda is the reason we did not win the election more decisively. If they had had their way we would be into our fourth term of opposition.

Organisational and campaigning changes also help to account for the party's progress. David Cameron accepted the need to devote proper resources and relentless focus to the ground war in target seats. Candidates were selected as early as possible. The Cameron Direct initiative enabled thousands of voters to listen to David and ask him questions in their home town. Direct mail was allowed to form a substantial part of the campaign budget, allowing detailed planning and innovative approaches like personalised postcards and the final week "contract". The fundraising operation widened our donor base and put the party in a strong position to fight the next election, whenever it comes.

WHY DID WE FAIL to win an overall majority in the House of Commons against a government so abjectly unpopular that it could muster no more than 29 per cent of the vote, only one point better than Michael Foot's Labour Party of 1983? Because we did not demonstrate that we were the change people wanted. At a national level, too much of our message was focused on Gordon Brown and Labour, not only in the weeks before the election but in the years before that. At best, this could only remind voters of the need for change, something they had long since decided for themselves; at worst, it suggested that we had little to say about our own plans, or were deliberately hiding them. In the post-expenses world, our attacks painted us as being part of the old politics that people longed to leave behind. When we asked people to vote for change we did not fully convey to them what sort of change we had in mind or how we would achieve it. Voters were puzzled by the theme of the Big Society, and though they had noticed a number of individual policies, they could not identify what tangible change we would bring. We took for granted, wrongly, that we would be the default choice for voters who deserted Labour; not having established ourselves decisively as the party of change, we allowed the Liberal

Democrats to take their chance in the televised debates. The fact that we did not complete the transformation of the brand meant that Labour scares about our plans, drawing on caricature folk memories of previous Conservative governments, had more resonance than they would otherwise have done. We spent too much of our campaign budget on the blunt instrument of billboard posters at the expense of additional targeted direct mail, and compounded the mistake by devoting much of the available space to redundant and counterproductive attacks on Gordon Brown. The very positive "Never voted Tory before" poster campaign was a good and well-executed idea but felt strangely detached from the rest of the Conservative message. Research was used inconsistently, with some messages and creative ideas tested in great detail while the bigger strategic imperative – the need to narrow the chasm between disillusionment with Labour and positive support for us – was neglected. Ultimately, we did not make as much progress as we should have done in reassuring nervous former Labour voters that we had changed and we were on their side.

Much earlier in the parliament, voters suspected there was a gap between David Cameron and the old Conservative Party which they worried would re-emerge if it found itself in government. That suspicion remained until polling day. Now we have the chance to prove they need not have feared.

Coda: the coalition

Some, including some Conservative MPs, have argued that rather than going into coalition with the Liberal Democrats, David Cameron ought to have gone it alone and formed a minority administration. He did acknowledge, on the day after polling day, the possibility of coming to a supply and confidence arrangement, in which the Liberal Democrats agreed to support a minority Conservative government in confidence motions and allowed it to pass its Budgets, but this was not his preference: it might be possible "to have a stronger, more stable, more collaborative government than that".[167] The Liberal Democrats were clearly keen to share power, and once the Conservative leader had made his "big, open and comprehensive offer" to the party, saying he wanted to "work together in tackling our country's big and urgent problems" and that he saw "a strong basis for a strong

167   David Cameron speech at St Stephen's Club, news.bbc.co.uk, 7 May 2010

government", it would have been very hard to change his tone and ask the Lib Dems to support a Conservative administration trying to govern alone.

The most likely alternative to a Conservative coalition with the Liberal Democrats was not a minority Conservative government but a Liberal Democrat deal with Labour. Spurious psephological evidence was called to support the contention that this was in fact the people's will. Caroline Lucas, the new Green MP for Brighton Pavilion, was not alone in claiming that this would be the most legitimate outcome because "far more people voted for a combination of the Liberal Democrats and Labour than for the Conservatives".[168] But this is the sort of argument you can only make if you have no sense of irony: in her constituency far more people voted for a combination of the Liberal Democrats and Labour than for her. Does she regard her own election as illegitimate?

The idea that the total of Labour and Liberal Democrat votes combined proved that Britain had wanted the two parties to form a government was pedalled hard by some on the left. Polly Toynbee argued that the two were "near-identical progressive parties, divided only by history, tradition and a rotten voting system", and that a Labour-Lib Dem coalition would be a "legitimate coalition of the voters' expressed wishes".[169] Ms Toynbee gives the impression that votes for the two parties were effectively interchangeable, as if they had fought the election on some sort of joint platform. The idea is ridiculous. For all Gordon Brown's claims during the television debates that he agreed with Nick, in many central areas of policy they were miles apart. The Liberal Democrats had long been fierce critics of Labour's economic policies, particularly the reliance on debt, both public and private; they had always opposed Labour's authoritarian agenda, from identity cards to detention without trial; they did not share Labour's approach to the NHS and promised to scrap the central targets that had been an essential part of the government's health policy; and they bitterly condemned the government's record on foreign affairs. In many areas, including civil liberties and school reform, Liberal Democrat ideas had more in common with those of the Conservatives than with Labour.

In spite of the natural alliance claimed for the two parties in some quarters, the talks that took place between Labour and the Liberal Democrats evidently did not go at all well, with Liberal Democrat sources complaining that Labour did not take them seriously and

168   *Today*, BBC Radio 4, 11 May 2010
169   'Lib-Lab – the only legitimate coalition', *Guardian*, 10 May 2010

Labour sources saying the Lib Dems already seemed to have made up their minds to go with David Cameron. But by the time these talks started on 10 May, three days after Mr Cameron's public offer of a coalition, it was clear that the Lib Dems' negotiations with the Conservatives were making real progress. Who knows what would have happened if David Cameron had made no big, open, comprehensive offer, and Nick Clegg's team had found the Tories unwilling to countenance sharing power? Surely both Labour and the Liberal Democrats would have taken the prospect of a deal more seriously and worked harder to achieve one.

But even if the stars had aligned in such a way as to make a minority Conservative government a real possibility, the choice David Cameron made to enter a coalition would still have been the right one, both for the country and for the Conservative Party. We had argued throughout the campaign that Britain needed a strong, stable government (in the cause of trying to avoid a hung parliament, ironically enough), and we were right. Whatever the advantages of a minority Conservative government may have been – and there are not many, since many parts of the Conservative manifesto that were put on hold in the coalition deal would only have got 306 votes in the Commons – such a government would probably not have been stable, and it certainly would not have been strong. Instead we have a coalition with a majority of 76 that promises to be both.

David Cameron's decision was also the right one for the Conservative Party, and not just because the coalition provides some political cover for tough decisions on tax and spending. Entering a coalition government has given the party the opportunity to complete the rehabilitation of the Conservative brand that is essential if we are to achieve an overall majority at future elections. The very fact of the coalition, and the way David and his team conducted themselves during the negotiations, suggested that we were concerned first and foremost with the national interest – something many sceptical voters would not have expected of us. The offer to work with the Liberal Democrats, and the Conservatives' grown-up demeanour in those uncertain days, were dramatically at odds with the public view of politicians as childish partisans, sniping and carping and scoring cheap points.

In our research throughout the parliament, when we showed swing voters a Conservative proposal or a clip of David Cameron speaking, they would often say something like, "Well, it sounds good and I want to believe it, but can I trust them? How do I know they'll do what they say?" Asked how the party could prove that it could indeed be trusted, more often than not they would say "by doing it". To be fair to the participants, they recognised how unreasonable this was – clearly a party could not deliver on its election promises before it was elected. But the point stands that many of those who voted Conservative did so with varying degrees of doubt or even trepidation, and many more thought about doing so but found their reservations too strong. However over-the-top the Labour scares about Tory plans, too many people thought they contained a kernel of truth.

It is only in government, then, that the Conservative Party can show doubtful voters that it really is on the side of ordinary people, that it is competent to run the economy, that it can be trusted with the NHS, that it is a change for the better. Could the Conservatives have shown all these things in a minority administration? It would have been very much more difficult. With unpopular decisions to be taken and tough measures to get through parliament, the government might soon have been struggling to survive from one month – or even one vote – to the next. Far from enacting the change we promised, or putting over any kind of vision, we would be reminding voters of the last Conservative government waiting to be put out of its misery.

Not only that, we would have rejected publicly the chance to form the strong, stable government we had been saying was essential, apparently in order to hoard power for the Conservative Party, whatever the consequences for the country. We would have missed the chance to keep another promise that voters expected us to break – to change politics.

Through his disappointment, David Cameron saw all this in the early hours of a Friday morning after a sleepless 36-hour whistle-stop tour and weeks of unimaginable pressure. Of his many qualities, the one that will serve him best as Prime Minister is his judgment. From the day he was elected leader, he has in the main made the right calls when it mattered most. In doing so he has rescued the Conservative Party. There is more to do, but since December 2005 the party has been heading in the right direction and at the time of writing it still is. Had David Cameron not grasped what needed to be done, the Conservative Party would be contemplating at least five more long years of opposition. Instead it is in government, and a newly elected Conservative Prime Minister has walked into 10 Downing Street for the first time in eighteen years.

As for the future, an apparently secure Commons majority for the coalition government does not make predictions any easier. In fact I believe the next few years will turn out to be even more intriguing than those we have just lived through. Will the coalition follow through on its promising start and retain public support even as budget cuts hit home? If things go well, which party will get the credit – and if they go badly, which will get the blame? How long will left-leaning Liberal Democrat MPs and activists tolerate the decline in their party's support (down to 12 per cent in a YouGov[170] poll on 1 August 2010, half their general election vote share)? Could we see defections on a bigger scale than in any recent parliament? Or will the Liberal Democrats manage to capitalise on their role in government and increase their support? Will the Conservative Party manage to reassure doubters that it can be trusted to govern in the interests of the whole country? Will the Labour Party learn from its defeat and be a real force at the next election, or will it turn away from reality and relevance? Will the country vote for electoral reform? If it does, how will it change election campaigning, and what will be the effect when combined with boundary changes? If it does not, how will Liberal Democrat demoralisation affect the coalition? Will we see electoral pacts – formal or otherwise – and what will be their long term consequences? What events – Donald Rumsfeld's unknown unknowns – lie in wait to test our rulers?

And what will the voters make of it all?

170   YouGov poll for the *Sunday Times*, 29-30 July 2010, sample 1,885

Appendix /
Selected published polls, 2005-2010

1. Voting intention monthly average, June 2005 to 6 May 2010 (ICM, Populus, YouGov)

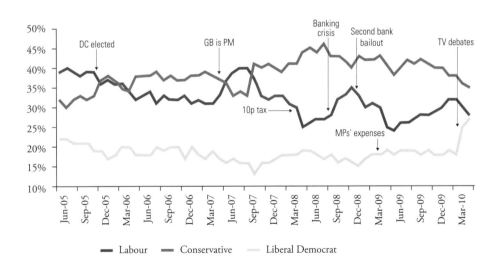

2. "With Britain's economy facing problems in the months ahead, who do you most trust to manage the economy in the best interests of Britain?" (Populus-*Times*)

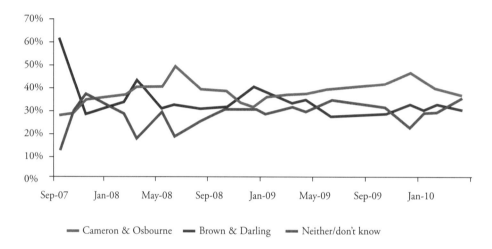

3. "Irrespective of which party you yourself support, which team do you think is better able to manage the economy properly – Gordon Brown and Alistair Darling, or David Cameron and George Osborne?" (ICM-*Guardian*, *Sunday Mirror*)

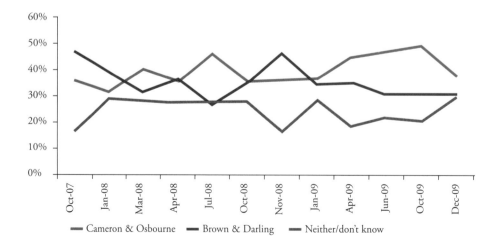

4. Putting aside your party preference, which of the three main party leaders do you feel would make the best Prime Minister right now, to deal with the economy in recession? (Populus-*Times*)

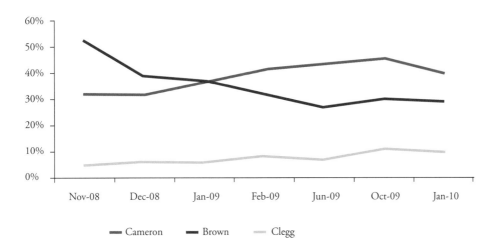

...the best Prime Minister to lead Britain forward after the general election?

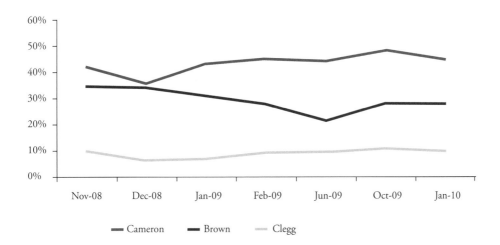

Do you think Gordon Brown is doing well or badly as Prime Minister / David Cameron is doing well or badly as Conservative leader / Nick Clegg is doing well or badly as leader of the Liberal Democrats? (YouGov-*Sunday Times*)

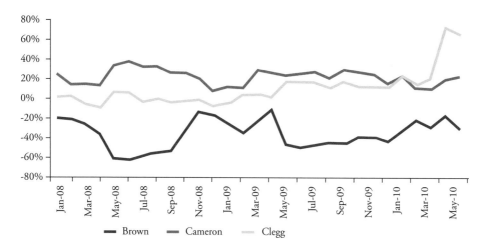

Net scores shown

Which of these would make the best Prime Minister? (YouGov/*Telegraph, Sun*)

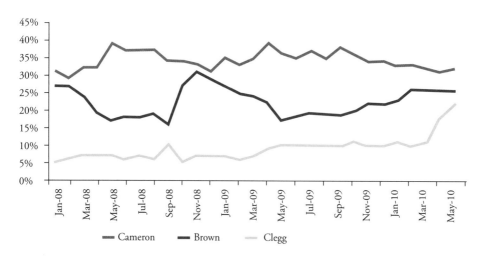

About the author

LORD ASHCROFT, KCMG, is an international businessman, author and philanthropist. He is Deputy Chairman of the Conservative Party in the UK and is also Treasurer of the International Democratic Union. He is also the founder and Chairman of the Board of Trustees of Crimestoppers, the only UK charity dedicated to solving crimes, Vice-Patron of the Intelligence Corps Museum, Trustee of the Imperial War Museum Foundation, Chairman of the Trustees of Ashcroft Technology Academy and Chancellor of Anglia Ruskin University.

Lord Ashcroft has a life-long interest in bravery and gallantry medals. In 1986, he started collecting Victoria Crosses. There are now more than 160 in his collection, estimated to be worth some £30 million, making it the largest collection of VCs in the world. In the autumn of 2010, the collection is due to go on public display for the first time at the Imperial War Museum in London. The new Lord Ashcroft Gallery, paid for by his £5 million donation, will also exhibit Victoria Crosses and George Crosses already belonging to or in the care of the IWM.

Lord Ashcroft has written six books:

- *George Cross Heroes*
- *Minority Verdict: The Conservative Party, the Voters and the 2010 Election*
- *Special Forces Heroes*
- *Victoria Cross Heroes*
- *Dirty Politics Dirty Times*
- *Smell the Coffee: A Wake-Up Call for the Conservative Party*

For more information visit:
- www.lordashcroft.com
- www.georgecrossheroes.com
- www.specialforcesheroes.com
- www.victoriacrossheroes.com